D1008786

ROBLOX

R⬛BL⬛X

Written by Alex Wiltshire
Edited by Craig Jelley
Designed by John Stuckey and Ian Pollard
Illustrations by Matt Burgess, John Stuckey and Ryan Marsh
Production by Louis Harvey
Special thanks to the entire Roblox team

All stats featured in this book were based on information publicly available on the Roblox platform and were correct as of March 2019.

ISBN 978-0-06-295016-1
❖
19 20 21 22 23   RTLO   10 9 8 7 6 5 4 3 2
First US Edition, 2019

Original English language edition first published in 2019 by Egmont UK Limited, The Yellow Building, 1 Nicholas Road, London, W11 4AN, United Kingdom.

Stay safe online. Any website addresses listed in this book are correct at the time of going to print. However, HarperCollins is not responsible for content hosted by third parties. Please be aware that online content can be subject to change and websites can contain content that is unsuitable for children. We advise that all children are supervised when using the internet.

ROBL✖X
TOP BATTLE GAMES

HARPER
An Imprint of HarperCollins*Publishers*

CONTENTS

HELLO!

GREETINGS, HUMAN

The cause of the Korblox Empire is bleak and you seem like just the type of warrior who might be able to increase the might of our ranks. Yes, you're much more powerful than other humans I've encountered. Tell me, do you have a desire to beat your enemies in battle? To defeat all competitors until you're the last one standing? Good. Very good. Then I may indeed be able to use you.

To become a member of the Korbloxian forces is a great honor. You'll need to prove your worth before you're let loose against the Redcliff blight, so I've collected here a gauntlet of battle games for you to prove your physical, mental, and tactical prowess. You'll need to defeat armed foes in arena combat, outwit the legions sent to infiltrate your bases, and rule the battlefield like so many great Korblox commanders have before you.

And with that, your challenge has been set. You must defeat all opponents along the way and ensure you master each game. If you prevail, you will become an integral part of the Korblox military. If you fail... well, you wouldn't want to disappoint us. Good luck, human.

KORBLOX GENERAL

PHANTOM FORCES

Choose your loadout, customize your gear, and deploy into this intense and detailed team-based shooter. With four classes to play as, over 10 maps to gun across, more weapons than a small army can handle, and three game modes to master, there's a world of action to get into!

Phantom Forces features three game modes, like Team Deathmatch, in which your squad must take out the opposition, or the exciting Flare Domination, where you'll capture and hold points across the map to win points for your team.

As you take out the enemy, capture points, and assist your team, you'll gain Ranks – a mark of your experience. Each Rank unlocks new weapons and attachments and also awards Credit, which you can spend on specific weapon unlocks.

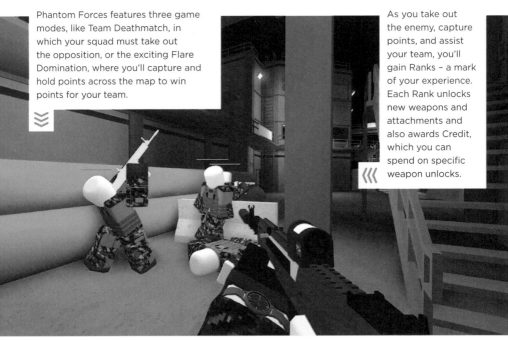

You can respawn beside any teammate. Watch them play for a while before hitting "Deploy" to identify the threats they're facing. Pick your moment carefully because you can't deploy on teammates in combat!

GAME STATS

STUDIO:	StyLiS Studios
SUBGENRES:	FPS, PvP
VISITS:	
FAVORITED:	

QUICK TIPS

ACCURACY
Firing a gun creates recoil, which will make your bullet spray increasingly inaccurate over a long period of time. Use quick, sharp bursts to create sustained damage over a short period of time and repeat over and over.

ART OF NOISE
Sound can be your friend or your enemy! You can listen for footsteps, including the various sounds different surfaces will make when walked on. Crouch to move quietly, and add a suppressor to silence your shots.

SPOTTING ENEMIES
When you see an enemy, don't be so quick to pull the trigger. Press the "spot" button while looking at an enemy to show them on the minimap. You'll earn XP and it gives your team the chance to get revenge if you are defeated.

QUICK RELOAD
Get in the habit of reloading whenever you can, but especially before the magazine is empty. This will maximize your downtime between battles and you'll find that reloading an empty gun takes slightly longer.

LITOZINNAMON

When a game you've made gets popular, it tends to take on a life of its own. That's true of Phantom Forces, which presented litozinnamon with some problems, such as how to deal with players exploiting glitches. Here, he explains the challenges he faced and how his game has grown over the years!

ON SCALE
When it was released, litozinnamon expected Phantom Forces to be popular, but it turned out to be even bigger than he hoped! "We didn't realize the significance of Roblox's growth in the past years," he says. "It's common to have tens of thousands of players at a time, something we never thought possible when we started."

ON GLITCHES
When litozinnamon saw players using movement glitches, he was surprised. "They allowed a player to get an extra jump or boost in midair

because of some flaws in our logic handling for dolphin-diving and sliding mechanics," he explains. "Needless to say, players actively wanted us to keep these glitches in the game, claiming that being able to pull off the key combinations to get them was a part of the skill that made the game unique and enjoyable."

ON HACKERS
He faced another unforeseen challenge: "I wish I knew our game would get large enough that a ton of people would try to hack it, so we would have known to put more thought into security."

DODGEBALL!

Dodgeball! is the classic game of hit or be hit! Two teams of up to six players compete to throw balls at each other to score KOs until no one on the opposing team is left standing. Keep an eye on your stock of balls, aim carefully, keep moving, and try not to be a target!

The red and blue teams start a match facing each other across the basketball court. You can't run into the opposing half, but you can throw balls into it. If you hit a rival, you'll hear a bell sound.

You get a stock of just four balls to throw at the start of a match, but you can pick up more from the field. Any ball that's red is safe to collect; avoid any ball that's white!

If you're hit four times in a match, you'll be knocked out and sent to the sidelines to watch the rest of the game play out. The game's over when a team has no players left.

You get Certz for hitting players and just taking part in matches, but you get the most for scoring KOs and for winning games. Exchange them in the shop for new outfits.

GAME STATS

DEVELOPER:	Alexnewtron
SUBGENRES:	Sports, Simulation
VISITS:	
FAVORITED:	

QUICK TIPS

STAY ON TARGET
If you're having trouble hitting opponents, try throwing towards the spot where players are running, not directly at them. Your throwing speed is slow. If you aim for where a player is, they'll be gone when the ball arrives.

COVER ME
If you're low on hitpoints, consider hanging around at the back of the court. That way other players on your side will provide cover from incoming balls and the other team can't target you. It's easier to collect new balls too.

DUCK AND DIVE
Once numbers are thinned out towards the end of a match, it gets easier to see incoming balls and dodge them. However, if your team is losing, it can mean you're the sole target. Make sure you practice dodging!

NEW BALLS
Some balls in the shop have special abilities. The Paintball briefly covers its victim's screen and the Bowling Ball makes them dizzy. Remember that the opposition can throw them right back again!

ALEXNEWTRON

Alexnewtron has made many hit Roblox games since he started out playing early classics like Work at a Pizza Place and Down Hill Smash! with his friends. Here, he shares some veteran advice on how to make games as well as he does, and why he loves the Roblox Developers Conference.

ON GETTING TOGETHER
For Alexnewtron, the best thing about being part of the Roblox community is getting to go to the annual Roblox Developers Conference! "It's always fun to go to RDC where I'm able to see my friends each year, and learn from the different teams at Roblox."

ON BEING ROUGH AND READY
"Don't try to make your game look perfect when you start making it," advises Alexnewtron. "It's easy to imagine in your head what you want your game to look and feel like, so you spend a lot of time polishing and developing an aesthetic before you even know if people want to play it. I learned it's important to create a functional game, even if it's ugly, to learn and understand how players play your game, before polishing."

ON ORGANIZATION
When you're as experienced as Alexnewtron, you'll know that being neat is just as vital a skill as scripting. "I always try to keep my objects in Roblox Studio as organized as possible, with lots of different folders that keep my assets ready to replicate to players as they join my game."

FLEE THE FACILITY

The experiments were meant to be secret. That was until they went wrong and a monstrosity managed to escape! Play a frantic game of survival as one of three desperate Survivors who are attempting to flee, or as the fearsome Beast that's trying to stop them!

To escape the facility, the Survivors must hack at least four of the six computers found in various rooms. But beware – hacking can take quite some time and it makes noise that will reveal your location to the Beast.

As the Beast, you must find and knock out each of the Survivors, then drag them to a cryo tube to freeze them. You only get a short time before they regain consciousness, and until their friends can save them before they freeze!

Survivors have no way of defeating the Beast, but they can crouch to use vents, which are a great way of avoiding obvious entry points. They can also hide in several lockers and other scene objects.

GAME STATS

STUDIO:	A. W. Apps
SUBGENRES:	Horror, Escape
VISITS:	
FAVORITED:	

QUICK TIPS

SCOUT OUT
It's a good idea to spend a lot of time learning the maps. Whether you're a Survivor or the Beast, you'll do a lot better if you can remember where the computers and cryogenic tubes are, because they're crucial to winning.

BREAK CAMP
It's tempting for the Beast to stay near a computer to catch Survivors when they come near, but there's no guarantee they won't just go and hack a different one. It's much more effective if the Beast does a circuit of all the computers.

HEAR THE BEAT
The Beast has a very strong heart. So strong, in fact, that you can hear it beating whenever it's lurking nearby! Survivors should listen for a pounding sound so that they know when it's safe to make a break for it.

CREEPY
The cabin in the lobby area houses a hidden secret. Sneak around the back to find a little hole in the wall, crawl through and navigate the maze to find a basement, which houses some mysterious arcade cabinets. Weird.

MRWINDY

After several years of making Roblox games, MrWindy has collected lots of experience. He knows that every developer faces slightly different challenges, but here he shares some super-useful skills he's learned which might make all the difference to you if you learn them, too!

ON INNOVATION
MrWindy suggests making games that you're passionate about. "I like to make games with unique gameplay that I would love to play with others and they would enjoy playing too. It's hard to finish a game you don't like working on."

ON SKILLS
"I try to work with my strengths and what I'm willing to learn," he says on the topic of keeping games manageable. "I don't want to feel discouraged and not finish a game because I'm not good at a particular skill."

ON STAMINA
His top tip for game development is one that not enough devs heed. "Pace yourself. Game development is a long and complicated process; it's a marathon, not a sprint. I like to split my game into small tasks to complete each day."

ON FAILURE
And for a final tip, MrWindy suggests: "Failure is not the end. It is a step in the learning process. Just as you don't quit playing a video game after a game over, you learn from your mistakes, pick up the controller, and keep playing."

LUCKY BLOCK BATTLEGROUNDS

Have you ever wished you could launch a killer whale at your enemies? Do you dream of hitting them with a pizza? How about rigging a lab bench to blow up in their faces? Lucky Block Battlegrounds is a game where you can never guess what weapon you'll be fighting with next!

You'll start at your base with access to one golden lucky block. Walk into it, then use the block in your inventory to get a random weapon.

A second golden block will unlock after 10 minutes. After 30, you'll start getting super blocks, which drop better gear. Then the rarer diamond blocks open after an hour!

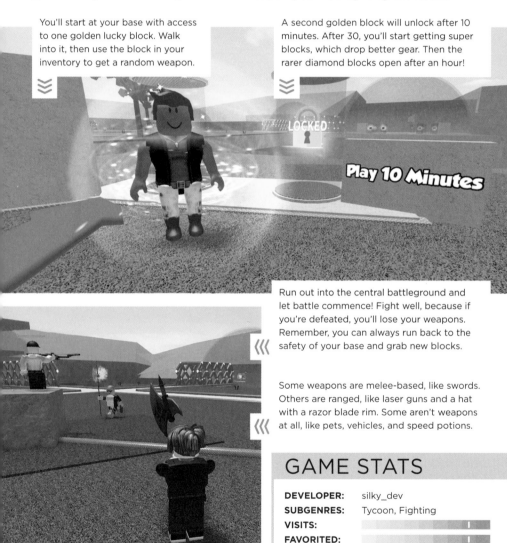

LOCKED

Play 10 Minutes

Run out into the central battleground and let battle commence! Fight well, because if you're defeated, you'll lose your weapons. Remember, you can always run back to the safety of your base and grab new blocks.

Some weapons are melee-based, like swords. Others are ranged, like laser guns and a hat with a razor blade rim. Some aren't weapons at all, like pets, vehicles, and speed potions.

GAME STATS

DEVELOPER: silky_dev
SUBGENRES: Tycoon, Fighting
VISITS:
FAVORITED:

QUICK TIPS

TEST CASE
Because most of your weapons will be completely new to you, it's a good idea to try using them before you leave the safety of your base so you can familiarize yourself with how they work and how to use them!

ESCAPE ARTIST
If you're near an enemy base and you're about to be defeated, there's a handy way to escape danger – run directly into the base! You'll be teleported to the middle of the battleground, closer to your HQ.

DOUBLE TROUBLE
Some weapons you unlock will have two different attacks. For example, the golden sword and shield have the ability to hit players normally and can also transform you into a flying spark so you can shock your enemies!

TIME CUBE
The weapons you get from lucky blocks are completely random. The longer you play, the more blocks you'll unlock, and the better the chance you'll get to find good, insane weapons like axe-wielding imp launchers.

SILKY_DEV

Lucky Block Battlegrounds started out as a side project, but after it became a hit, silky_dev realized it deserved more attention! Here, he explains how being persistent helps him overcome the development problems he often comes up against, and why gameplay always comes first.

ON DETERMINATION
Persistence is silky_dev's key skill. "Being determined when developing has helped me complete my projects," he says. "Often I've hit challenges along the way that have really made me want to quit. However, I learned to stick with it and finish strong. It really pays off in the end."

ON PUTTING GAMEPLAY FIRST
When silky_dev started out, he'd tend to focus on complex details like monetization and interface design, "and not enough on solid gameplay mechanics," he says. "To create a successful game, I should first focus on creating a fun experience. I think it is important to focus first on that to draw your users back."

ON BATTLE STRATEGIES
He would never have thought of some of the ways that players fight in his game. "I underestimated the battle strategies people would come up with!" he says. "For example, some friends will work together and form a team to dominate the battlegrounds. If you aren't careful you could easily get surrounded by a powerful team."

SUPER BOMB SURVIVAL

It's raining bombs! How you survive the disasters that you're about to face is up to you. You can avoid them with skills that give you a super jump or a speedy sprint, or you can join in, taking out your competitors with your own bombs. Just try to keep your head!

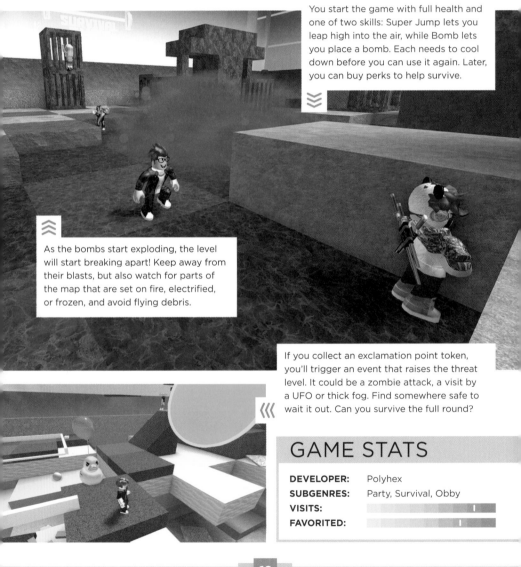

You start the game with full health and one of two skills: Super Jump lets you leap high into the air, while Bomb lets you place a bomb. Each needs to cool down before you can use it again. Later, you can buy perks to help survive.

As the bombs start exploding, the level will start breaking apart! Keep away from their blasts, but also watch for parts of the map that are set on fire, electrified, or frozen, and avoid flying debris.

If you collect an exclamation point token, you'll trigger an event that raises the threat level. It could be a zombie attack, a visit by a UFO or thick fog. Find somewhere safe to wait it out. Can you survive the full round?

GAME STATS

DEVELOPER:	Polyhex
SUBGENRES:	Party, Survival, Obby
VISITS:	
FAVORITED:	

QUICK TIPS

LOAD OUT
Perks change the way you play. There are lots to select – from Unshakable, which prevents you from being knocked over, to Double Jump. They're available to buy from the shop with coins you earn through playing.

ABLE BODY
There are over 50 skills to buy and try out. As you play rounds and use them more, you'll level them up so they become even more powerful. Pick a strategy for surviving rounds and choose a skill that suits your plan.

LOOK OUT
As the round plays out, pickups will appear. Pizza restores your health and coins add to your pot to spend after the round ends, so they're often worth the risk of collecting them if they're not completely isolated.

COVER ME
Craters might look safe to hide in, but there's a layer of lava just beneath the surface, which will deplete your health if you fall in. Bombs will create even greater holes to the lava, so be increasingly vigilant with every bomb!

POLYHEX

Polyhex loved Roblox's physics from when he started playing, and so he was immediately drawn to making physics games – "destroying big structures with friends and just going wild with the possibilities." Here, he explains how Super Bomb Survival was all about recreating that feeling!

ON INFO
The most important resource for Polyhex is the API reference! "Inside is a page with an explanation for every object you'll find in Roblox Studio, their properties, functions, and events," he says. "Learning their unique uses is key to creating a Roblox game effectively."

ON EMERGENT STRATEGIES
"Super Bomb Survival has a wild amount of variables going on, so there are always people trying new things!" says Polyhex. "One of the funniest examples I can think of is when people

discovered using the Dive skill (an item that flings you across the map in a ragdoll) with the Unshakable perk (which prevents you from ragdolling) to launch themselves across the game at high speeds, while maintaining control."

ON SUCCESS
When he made SBS, Polyhex only saw it as a fun game. "It fit the niche of a goofy, low-stress arena game. I could never have imagined it getting this big, getting an official Roblox toy, or the overwhelming amount of love and support from the community I've had since its release!"

SKYWARS

Take your sword, pickaxe, and bow in hand, stash some blocks, and defend your island in the sky! It's up to you whether you build up your fortifications and let the enemy come to you, or set out for their islands and take the fight to them. Just try not to look down...

Each match begins with all eight players on their own tiny island in the sky. You can dig blocks with your pickaxe, place them to build structures and bridges, and fight with your sword or bow. 》》

Hidden in the ground are several kinds of ore blocks: coal, diamond, emerald, and gold, which you can mine by clearing blocks around them to earn coins. Spend them in the lobby on better gear and powerups.

Your game ends if you fall or you're killed, and you win if you survive to the end. Enemies will drop coins as they're defeated, and you'll earn a big bonus if you're the last player standing! 《《

GAME STATS

STUDIO:	16bitplay Games
SUBGENRES:	Crafting, Exploration, Building
VISITS:	
FAVORITED:	

QUICK TIPS

SCALE BUILDING
Getting good at building means that you can navigate the islands quickly and accurately, escape strong enemies, and create barriers between you and your opponents. Zoom out to get a bird's-eye view as you build.

RECON SWEEP
Keep a close eye on the other islands, and keep track of where your opponents are. Consider letting other players fight each other while you collect materials, then you can finish off the remaining players.

PICK A WEAPON
The pickaxe might not be the best weapon to use in melee combat, but if you're cunning enough it can be deadly. Use it to break the blocks your opponents are standing on to send them into the blue void below.

DRINK ME
Use the time between rounds to stock up on useful items from the lobby. You can buy health potions and shields to give yourself an edge in battle, or swig a high jump or speed potion to increase your agility.

0_0

0_0 has started making a lot of games, but he hasn't finished many of them. But even if they were never released, all those attempts gave him lots of knowledge that he's used on new ideas! Here, he explains how, and also shares some hot tips on top SKYWARS play!

ON COMPLETING
When you get an idea, it's easy to start making it. "I've probably made over 300 games but only a few of them are active on Roblox," says 0_0. "It can be challenging to finish developing them as I like to release them at a certain standard."

ON UPGRADING
0_0 recommends mining ore to buy the Stone Pickaxe. "It's a lot better than the default wooden one, it mines ore and blocks a lot faster," he says. "If someone has better gear and they charge towards you, you could try to use

your Stone Pickaxe to quickly mine below them to make them fall into the void!"

ON EXPERIENCE
Having made so many games, 0_0 has lots of experience to draw from! "I'm able to quickly refer back to my old projects," he says.

ON UNDERMINING
"Another good tip; when a player comes close, mine a block below, jump in the hole, and use your sword. This is good because you'll be below them so you can hit them but they can't hit you!"

REDWOOD PRISON

Play by the rules or break out for a life on the run? Enforce the law or go rogue? Patrol the prison perimeter in a police cruiser or mount a daring escape in a helicopter? Whether you play as a prisoner, the police, or a fugitive, the life you lead in Redwood Prison is up to you!

At the start of the game, you'll choose to play as police or prisoner. It's the police players' duty to make the prisoners obey the rules and prevent fugitives from causing a riot.

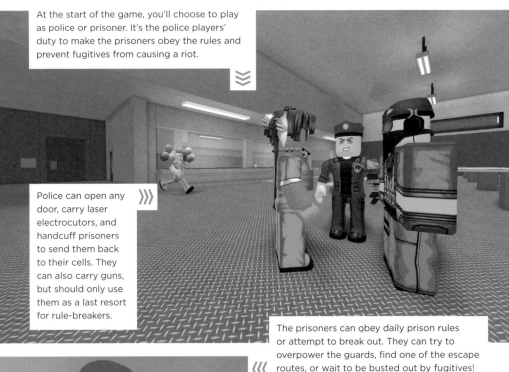

Police can open any door, carry laser electrocutors, and handcuff prisoners to send them back to their cells. They can also carry guns, but should only use them as a last resort for rule-breakers.

The prisoners can obey daily prison rules or attempt to break out. They can try to overpower the guards, find one of the escape routes, or wait to be busted out by fugitives!

Prisoners can escape to Walworth town, where they can hide out and collect supplies. They can also turn fugitive by walking on the yellow plate in the central tent.

GAME STATS

DEVELOPER:	RoyStanford
SUBGENRES:	Escape, Town and City
VISITS:	
FAVORITED:	

QUICK TIPS

FACE THE MUSIC
One way prisoners can escape is by finding a guitar on the prison grounds to give to an NPC called Trenton. If the police were smart enough to guard the instrument, they might have a higher criminal-catching success rate!

GOOD BEHAVIOR
Whether you play as police, prisoner, or fugitive, there are many chances to role-play. Set tasks for prisoners using the noticeboard in the cafeteria and punish them if they don't behave, or start a gang outside the prison walls.

GREAT POSTURE
The on-screen icon of the body reveals a menu of different stances you can use on your character. Prisoners can kneel, sit, have their hands cuffed behind them, and even play dead! Will they use these powers to comply or to deceive?

HIDEAWAY
You can enter any of the houses around the nearby town to take shelter from pursuing cops or other fugitives. With exits at the front and back of most houses, they're great for giving pursuers the slip and making a speedy getaway.

ROYSTANFORD

Making games can be tricky and mistakes can make you feel like giving up, but as RoyStanford explains, he won't let that stop him from wanting to make them, or from pushing himself to explore new kinds of designs! After all, he loves the surprise of seeing how people play his games.

ON TUNES
"A lot of aspects of developing can be tedious and time-consuming," says RoyStanford. "Listening to music helps me get more work done because it relaxes me."

ON MAKING MISTAKES
Even with his experience, RoyStanford says he still makes many mistakes. "It's impossible to make a game that is perfect, and when I first started, any issues or bugs used to discourage me. Luckily I kept trying, and with every project I got better and better. Don't give up!"

ON STORYTELLING
"I think it would be very fun to make a story-based adventure game, where you play with a squad of either two or four people. I think video games are an amazing way to tell stories, and I'd love the chance to make a compelling story myself," he says.

ON ROLE-PLAYING
"Players really make Redwood Prison their own game," says RoyStanford. "It's amazing to see players creating identities for themselves, such as a police officer who is actually undercover."

ELEMENTAL BATTLEGROUNDS

Attune yourself with screen-filling elemental magic, arm yourself with a book of spectacular spells, and enter immortal combat with 11 other players in Elemental Battlegrounds. Unleash your formidable powers on your enemy... but you'll need to be agile and quick to avoid theirs!

Equip yourself with a set of up to four spells you've learned. You start with three spells taken from an element of your choice. Casting consumes mana, which regenerates over time.

Casting spells and taking out other players earns experience points. When you level up, you'll be rewarded with Shards, Diamonds, and a Skill Point, all of which upgrade your stats and unlock new spells and elements.

The basic elements are Fire, Water, and Grass, but there are more to unlock, some by fusing elements. Each element has a different focus, so experiment with them all.

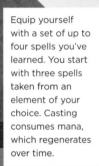

On each map there's a Drop Zone, where Diamonds and Shards will randomly appear. Be aware that these riches attract many players, so prepare yourself for a brawl!

GAME STATS

STUDIO:	Gamer Robot
SUBGENRES:	Fantasy, Fighting, Survival
VISITS:	
FAVORITED:	

QUICK TIPS

BLOCK & WEAVE
Avoid incoming attacks by double-tapping your jump or directional button to do flips and rolls that can bamboozle your opponents and throw off their aim. You can also hold down the block button to absorb any attacks!

COMBO BREAKER
Plan your skill loadout to combine the effects of different spells. Magic that stuns, for instance, is great when used with slow-casting spells, as you'll be able to charge them while your enemy is unable to escape.

DOUBLE UP
Team up with a friend to take control of the battlefield! Consider your shared loadouts so you can cast huge combos and time your attacks so that you're always disrupting your enemies and dealing damage together.

FINISHING MOVE
Ultimate spells are so powerful that they can turn a losing battle on its head. Be very careful to time them right as they have such long cooldowns that you won't be able to use them again for a little while.

MYGAME43

Elemental Battlegrounds has lots of secrets and a huge set of attack combos for you to explore. Mygame43 loves to watch players come to grips with all the features he's created. Here, he explains how they're the result of understanding what Roblox players want!

ON MARKET RESEARCH
"Our team has a secret weapon", says mygame43. "The master behind our game concepts is the famous Roblox player, Wenlocktoad. He truly has an understanding of what players are looking for in a new game."

ON EXPLORING
The game is filled with hidden locations: "If you find a hidden skull on our standard map, you will teleport to a creepy map that has a secret element that can only be used there. And there's an Easter egg on the Water map, which is the

entrance to the Water City, found below a large bridge outside the city."

ON COMBOS
Mygame43 likes to see how players use different attacks. "They find the most creative attack combos," he says. "And they always find new ways to create stronger combos!"

ON CANCELING OUT
"Starter elements can defuse each other", says mygame43. "For example, using Fire against Grass attacks will burn the Grass in mid-air!"

BE A PARKOUR NINJA

A ninja's weapons are both their sharpened blades and their sharpened wits, and that's what you'll need to be a master in Be a Parkour Ninja! Wait in the shadows for the perfect moment to strike, climb to a vantage point to attack at range, or rely on your incredible agility to prevail.

Start the match by equipping yourself with your sword of choice. The Katana delivers swift slashing blows, while the Heavy Sword takes a moment to charge before it unleashes a lethal spinning sweep.

You'll always have throwing daggers called Kunai, which allow you to fight at range, and a smoke bomb that cloaks the area in a white cloud, disorienting enemies so you can escape or attack them.

In this game, you're super-agile. You can dash in the air by double-tapping jump, scale sheer walls by jumping into them, and quickly dodge left and right.

Use the map to your advantage. Watch the action from a tall tower, or concealed in bushes. The best ninjas are patient and pick the right time to enter the battle!

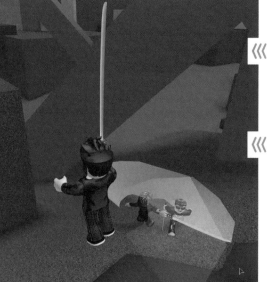

GAME STATS

DEVELOPER:	Aurarus
SUBGENRES:	Obby, Fighting
VISITS:	
FAVORITED:	

QUICK TIPS

FIVE IN A ROW
Killstreaks, defeating enemies without dying, aren't just good for your score. For every fifth takedown you'll get a health potion. They take time to consume and can attract attention, but might lead to even higher scores!

PRECISION EDGE
Your movement is slowed slightly for a second after each swing of your sword, so don't spam the same attacks over and over. You never know when you'll need to make a quick getaway and require your full movement range.

CLONE WAR
You also have the ability to summon a shadowy clone beside you when you dodge, which can prove very confusing for any enemies trying to hit you. Pair with a dropped smoke bomb to completely confound them!

HIGH ALERT
Kunai are very useful for attacking from a distance, even when hiding, but remember that your enemies will often hear and see them hitting the ground, which could give away your concealed position and draw enemies to you.

AURARUS

Sometimes ideas come from places you never expect. That's true of Be a Parkour Ninja, which was meant to be a way bigger game than it ended up being. But that, developer Aurarus says, is just how game development goes! And big ideas aren't always such a good idea anyway...

ON PROTOTYPING FAST
While it's good to have a strong idea for your game, Aurarus suggests being adaptable. "Quickly trying out different approaches with very loose scripts and set pieces might give you better ideas for how your final draft should be."

ON MISTAKES
"Bigger and more complex is not always better," says Aurarus, remembering how when he was starting out he'd make big baseplates because he wanted to make big games. "It turns out this approach kind of overwhelms you," he says.

"Most developers find success by slowly adding on to already complete experiences."

ON SURPRISE ORIGINS
Be a Parkour Ninja started as a tech demo for an open-world ninja MMO. "I was never expecting people to like it as much as they did, and continue to play it!"

ON ROBLOX
What's special about it? "I like how Roblox, even 10 years after playing, still feels like it has this large unexplored potential."

PRISON ROYALE

48 inmates enter. One leaves. Prison Royale is an intense competition to find the fittest survivor of San Cercili Prison. Parachute into a large open map, find the weapons and gear to give you the advantage, defeat all opponents, and maybe you'll be the one to come out on top.

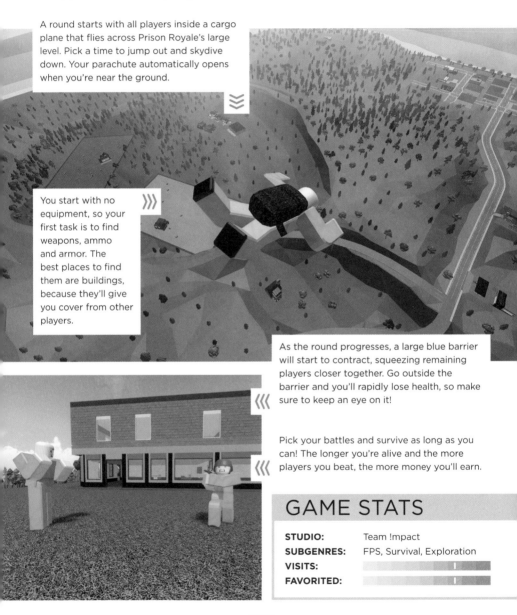

A round starts with all players inside a cargo plane that flies across Prison Royale's large level. Pick a time to jump out and skydive down. Your parachute automatically opens when you're near the ground.

You start with no equipment, so your first task is to find weapons, ammo and armor. The best places to find them are buildings, because they'll give you cover from other players.

As the round progresses, a large blue barrier will start to contract, squeezing remaining players closer together. Go outside the barrier and you'll rapidly lose health, so make sure to keep an eye on it!

Pick your battles and survive as long as you can! The longer you're alive and the more players you beat, the more money you'll earn.

GAME STATS

STUDIO:	Team !mpact
SUBGENRES:	FPS, Survival, Exploration
VISITS:	
FAVORITED:	

QUICK TIPS

FULL CLIP
Whenever you pick up a new weapon, it won't have any bullets, so don't forget to load it with ammo before you go charging into the middle of a gunfight! You definitely don't want to get caught with an empty magazine!

SAFE LANDING
As the cargo plane flies across the island, watch where your competitors head. You can follow the herd to instantly get into the action, or pick a quiet spot to stock up on weapons and supplies before looking for enemies.

BARRIER RACER
The barrier can be used to your advantage. If you stay close to it, you'll know that all your enemies are ahead of you. Be wary of how fast it can move, though – you might want to consider driving a buggy to outpace it!

LISTEN UP
Your ears are your most valuable assets, since footsteps and weapons will tell you other players are nearby. React to any sounds you hear to give yourself the advantage, but don't forget that you make noise too!

SCRIPTON

How do you make a game as big as Prison Royale? For ScriptOn, it's about helping himself concentrate and then focusing on the most important of the ideas behind it. It led to great success, but as he explains, he also had to accept that other players are way better than him!

ON FINDING THE FUN
"You can work hard on something but if the game isn't fun then it's all for nothing," he says. He advises making a minimum viable product first. "This means you make your game with only core mechanics in mind. Theoretically, once you finish it, your game should be fun. If not, you may need to go back to the drawing board."

ON BEING SECOND-BEST
When people started playing Prison Royale, ScriptOn had a big surprise. "After testing it every day for months and becoming an expert at the game, it was mind-blowing to watch someone else destroy me and other developers."

ON BEING PRODUCTIVE
ScriptOn has some tips to increase productivity. "Put on some relaxing music and make sure your environment is work-oriented. The more focused you are, the more productive you are."

ON FONDEST ROBLOX MEMORIES
"Probably waking up at 10 a.m. on a Saturday when I was 12 and playing Stickmasterluke's Underground War for a few hours."

NOTORIETY

Pulling off the heist of a lifetime was never going to be easy. But when you're faced with a full-on police assault and three minutes until your getaway van arrives, maybe, you think, the whole thing was a terrible mistake. Then again, it's all exactly what you and your team signed up for!

You can either join another player's heist or start one yourself. Some are free, but most cost money; the more you spend, the greater your cash and XP reward when you successfully escape. Ready your equipment, guns, and armor before deploying!

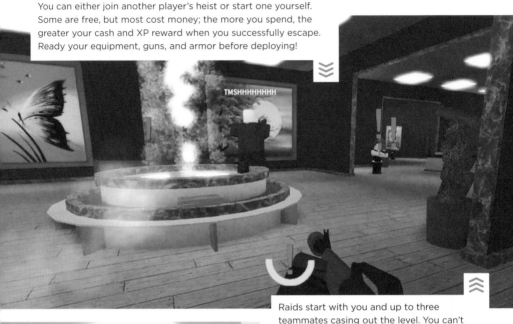

TMSHHHHHHHH

Raids start with you and up to three teammates casing out the level. You can't interact with anything yet, but if you can avoid alerting civilians, you'll be able to prepare a plan. Put on your mask to start!

Your objective is to steal a set amount of money, but once you're caught breaking the law, you have 30 seconds before the police arrive. Then the race is on to steal enough money before the whole team is taken out!

GAME STATS

DEVELOPER:	Brick_man
SUBGENRES:	FPS, Escape, Stealth
VISITS:	
FAVORITED:	

QUICK TIPS

SILENT NIGHT
You can "stealth" a heist by avoiding all alerts. Avoid being seen by cameras and guards, and don't make noises by using weapons or breaking glass. If civilians see you, you'll have to take them hostage before they raise an alarm.

ACT NORMAL
Your loadout can affect how easily you'll be detected. Avoid carrying big guns and wearing heavy armor to remain more inconspicuous. Use silencers if you have to shoot, and make sure no one sees any bodies...

ACCESS AREA
You can find keycards hidden around each level that enable you to access back rooms of shops, where more money is usually stored. You can only carry one large money bag at a time, and you can't sprint.

KNOW THE ENEMY
Police are equipped with different types of weapons and armor. Snipers aim from rooftops and SWAT teams can carry shields. Beware of the sneakiest cops, cloakers, who hide and can take you out in a single hit!

BRICK_MAN

For Brick_man, the joy of making games is about seeing how creative his players are. Here, he explains how much he values and enjoys listening to them, taking on their ideas, and seeing the incredible ways they take on the challenges he sets for them, often beyond what he intended!

ON LENDING AN EAR
What's a good skill to have as a Roblox developer? "Listening to the community," says Brick_man. "People always have great suggestions. I get dozens of messages every day with amazing ideas. Listening and acting on them ensures people are both happy and constantly entertained."

ON INGENUITY
Notoriety gives players lots of ways to achieve its goals, and that means Brick_man is constantly surprised by how they play.

"Sometimes they find ways to complete missions that I never anticipated. For example, the Mall Raid mission is supposed to only be completed with the police being called." But some players managed to not get caught!

ON NOT GETTING CAUGHT
Brick_man advises that you should avoid getting seen in Notoriety, because you get a 10% cash bonus! "Communicate with your team and make a plan before starting a heist. If people want to complete a mission stealthily, make sure everyone brings the right equipment!"

ULTIMATE BOXING

Take to the water in the ultimate seafaring vessel: the humble box. In Ultimate Boxing, you'll take your trusty box, which you can fully customize with weaponry and other upgrades, into battle with other 'boxers' to see who will be the last box standing... or floating.

If you're a little bit nervous about dipping your box in the water, then there are dozens of training drills for you to try out and improve your skills. Access them from the lobby area.

When you're ready, you can jump straight into one of three different game modes across a variety of maps: Free For All, Team Death Match, and King of the Sea. Each one will pit you in a competition against other box-sailing enemies.

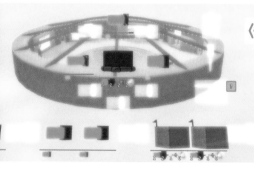

You can upgrade your box with a different box hull, and equip it with all sorts of parts that change the way you can attack other boats. You have eight slots to adapt your ship, so fill them all when you can.

GAME STATS

STUDIO:	Nexus Development
SUBGENRES:	Party, PvP, Humor
VISITS:	
FAVORITED:	

QUICK TIPS

RIGHT PART
With so many slots to fill to supplement your box's potential, you'll need to have a lot of parts to attach. You can buy parts from the Store in the lobby area, or purchase a crate, which will reward you with a random item to use.

SLOW TRAIN
Ultimate Boxing is a frantic battle game and it can be a little overwhelming to jump straight into a competitive game. The training modes all aim to help you perfect one area of the game, so work your way through them to improve.

STAT CHECKER
You can keep track of how well you've been playing by visiting the Stats section of the lobby. Here you'll be able to find your KOs (knockouts), WOs (wipeouts), and other facts like how many crates you've opened.

CRATE COLLECTOR
As well as being able to purchase them from the Store, you can also find crates hidden around some of the maps. Keep an eye out for pieces of wood floating around to save yourself a few hard-earned Robux.

THENEXUSAVENGER

Having grown up playing the likes of Jailbreak and Prop Hunt on Roblox with his friends, TheNexusAvenger made the jump to becoming a creator. Here, he reveals a few lessons he's learned from the games he's released, tells us how he felt his games have been received, and shows us what's on his horizon!

ON EARNED KNOWLEDGE
Not many developers start out with all the skills they need to create a game. TheNexusAvenger has seen improvements in his creations from game to game due to the things he's learned. "One thing I wish I knew when I started was how to make scalable UI for multiple platforms. Ultimate Boxing has a much stronger focus in this area."

ON RECEIVING ATTENTION
The Roblox community seems to have noticed the improvements in his games if their popularity is anything to go by. "Roblox Battle (2018 Edition) didn't get as much coverage as I expected, but for Ultimate Boxing, the reactions were better."

ON UPCOMING GAMES
TheNexusAvenger's collection of creations is due to expand in the near future too. "My next game is Project Dart Storm, a dart-based fighting game, and it will be another open-sourced game." He's even enlisting the help of an instructor of Nerf-focused physical education classes to advise on the project!

TINY TANKS

Lock and load! It's time to hop in a tank and trundle to the battlefield for this vehicular shoot-'em-up. You'll team up with a fleet of tanks to defeat an opposing battalion over a variety of frantic game modes set across a handful of minuscule maps.

Players are split up into teams of six, each controlling a miniature tank on a huge battlefield. The tanks range from the speedy Locust to the juggernaut Bastion. Each has its own pros and cons.

As you kill, capture, and win matches, you'll earn cash that can be used to upgrade your stats. You can choose from up to 20 different tanks in the Toybox at the start of a round.

You get to vote on the game mode and map you'll play next. Their are common modes like Deathmatch and Capture The Flag, as well as Domination, where you'll compete to keep hold of locations, and Regicide, where one player earns points as the king.

GAME STATS

DEVELOPER:	Sharksie
SUBGENRES:	Vehicles, PvP
VISITS:	
FAVORITED:	

QUICK TIPS

REBOUND

Aiming for enemies is all well and good, but these straight shots can be dodged easily if they're seen. All bullets will bounce at least once, so try to rebound them around corners and off walls to hit enemies in their hiding spots.

SPEEDY

Tank stats vary wildly, but the most important one to consider is its speed. It can be frustrating to spot a bullet heading in your direction and being too slow to avoid it. Choose speedy tanks whenever possible.

SECRET SKILLS

Every class has a secondary skill that they can deploy after a delay. These range from extra offensive moves, like laying mines, or more defensive maneuvers, such as building a wall to protect yourself and your team.

BARRAGE

You can only shoot a certain amount of bullets in a single burst, but they recharge over time. The best tactic is to release a volley whenever you have full ammo to increase the number that the enemy have to dodge. Fire away!

SHARKSIE

Before he joined up with AbstractAlex to create RedManta LLC, Sharksie was a prolific developer in his own right. Tiny Tanks was one of the first games he released and it's developed a cult following. Here, he talks to us about his collaborations and how he gets the most from his game ideas.

ON COLLABORATION

"It allows you to tackle projects that would be impossible to complete by yourself," Sharksie explains. "Having a diverse team allows you to get input from people with different backgrounds and experiences!"

ON EARLY PLAYING

"When a project has a long timeline, it can be hard to stay motivated the entire way through," he says. "This is why we like to make our games playable from an early stage. We can enjoy playing the game as we add to it!"

ON TIMING

"Making a game isn't easy," Sharksie reminds us. "It's easy to underestimate the time it takes to make a game. It's important to have good time management."

ON THE ULTIMATE GAME

With considerable experience and a successful team around him, what would Sharksie's dream game be? "One of our dream games is to create a large futuristic city where hundreds of players can own apartments in skyscrapers while roleplaying in the metropolis down below."

PROJECT: LAZER

Become a blaster master and jump into the stylish world of Project: Lazer, a crazy game of lazer-tag. Run, bounce, and shoot your way through the labyrinthine maps to eliminate your opponents and take your team to the top of the pile, or defeat all enemies for solo glory.

⋘ When you enter the game, you'll be dropped into the bright lobby, where you can choose which of the frantic game modes to play. At the moment, there are just two - Death Match and King of the Egg.

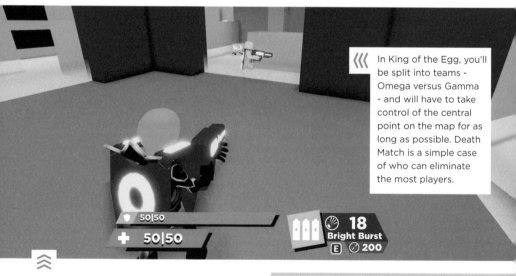

⋘ In King of the Egg, you'll be split into teams - Omega versus Gamma - and will have to take control of the central point on the map for as long as possible. Death Match is a simple case of who can eliminate the most players.

In each game mode, you'll see power-ups lying around - these range from shields to boost your defenses, to ammo and different types of weapons. Make sure you grab any you see to keep you in the game for longer.

GAME STATS

STUDIO:	A.W. Apps
SUBGENRES:	FPS, PvP, Sci-Fi
VISITS:	
FAVORITED:	

QUICK TIPS

JUMP INTO BATTLE
The maps that host the Project: Lazer battles are full of twists, turns, bridges, and ledges to use to your advantage. Making your way around can be difficult, but the green jump pads make reaching hidden areas easy.

PICK YOUR AMMO
You start every match with the basic Assault Blaster ammo, but there are pick-ups around the map that can change the way your gun fires. Ammo like Bright Burst gives you a wide shotgun-like spread, for example.

PRECIOUS HEALTH
There aren't any items on the battlefield that will replenish your health, so make sure to pick up any shield boost you can find. If you stop taking fire, your health will automatically regenerate after a while, but slowly.

SPEED BOOST
Being eliminated over and over again can be annoying. Luckily, when you respawn you get a temporary shield that blocks all bullets. Use this brief invincibility to collect ammo and shields before going into battle again.

MRWINDY

The creator of this neon-splashed shooter is MrWindy, who released the game through his studio, A.W. Apps. Here, he discusses the skills he's learned over his fledgling career, what he finds difficult in game development, and his views on the games that other creators produce.

ON TIME-TAUGHT LESSONS
MrWindy says that, in his earliest days as a programmer, "I wish I had known more about the networking design of online games on Roblox." That's why he worked hard to expand his skills and create an excellent multiplayer experience, proving that continuous learning is an essential part of game development.

ON STARTING A GAME
One aspect of development that MrWindy finds tricky is designing the core game mechanic and how it can be implemented on Roblox.

However, some things are easier for him: "It's easy for me to program and make the rest of the game once I have all of the planning and designing done."

ON LEARNING FROM OTHERS
Like most devs on Roblox, he feels the community is one of the best aspects, both in terms of the players and other developers. "I love talking to other devs and seeing their creativity. Roblox gives everyone these great tools and it's amazing watching people take these tools and push the platform to its limits and beyond."

PARKOUR TAG!

The wind in your hair, the thrill of the chase... Parkour Tag! is the fastest game of tag you've ever played! Two teams take turns to be the runners and taggers in massive open levels of platforms and tunnels. Parkour to evade your pursuers and Triple Jump to take your opponent by surprise.

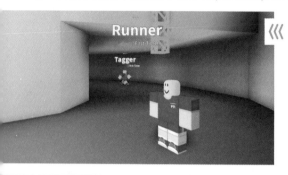

One team, either red or blue, will start out as the taggers. For the next minute, their task is to touch as many of the opposite team as possible. For each tag, the team is awarded a point.

After a minute, the tagger team becomes the runner team. It's time to run away! Use your Triple Jump, Sprint, and Trap skills to keep out of reach. After four minute-long rounds, the team with the most tags wins!

Hit jump three times in a row to Triple Jump, which is a great way to access far-off platforms or high towers. Sprint is a quick speed boost. Both skills have a cooldown period.

If your Trap skill is ready when you run over triggers on the floor, walls will open or close up, or bridges will appear or disappear, helping you shake a tagger off your tail. Keep your eye out for them!

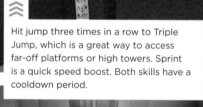

GAME STATS

DEVELOPER:	AznDibs
SUBGENRES:	Obby, PvP
VISITS:	
FAVORITED:	

QUICK TIPS

SPREAD IT
Infection is an alternative game mode, where one player starts off infected. When they touch others, they'll turn infected as well. The runners win if they can survive two minutes without being turned to the green side!

PICK A RUNNER
You can choose between four different classes to play. Normal Bob is balanced, while each of the others boosts a certain skill. For example, the Leaper is an agile class with an increased jumping ability.

TURN TABLES
When the countdown appears, it's the perfect time to plan a sneaky tag. When the countdown runs out, roles will switch. If you are about to become a tagger, turn right back on your pursuers to tag them by surprise!

MONEY HAT
You're rewarded coins for tags you make and wins your team earns. Convert your currency into customizations for your avatar, including hats, faces, and other gear to make your runner as intimidating or speedy as possible.

AZNDIBS

Before Parkour Tag!, AznDibs was used to getting just a couple of hundred visits to his games. But then a YouTuber streamed Parkour Tag! and it started getting noticed by the community! Here, he explains the value of working on a team, and balancing development with life.

ON WORKING TOGETHER
AznDibs has learned that collaboration helps speed up projects. "When I first started out, I sought to create all aspects of my games," he says. "While this is achievable, I found that I enjoy certain aspects of game development and I'm more productive working on them."

ON WORK-LIFE BALANCE
"Juggling game development with school, work and daily life is tough," says AznDibs. "What keeps me going is seeing the community enjoy and express themselves in my games."

ON DANCING
AznDibs added a feature to complement the behavior he saw being used in the game. "A portable disco floor pops up if three people are dancing together. It's hilarious to see during a hectic match!"

ON PLAYING IT RIGHT
"The best moments of playing on Roblox for me are when my friends and I play games not exactly as they are intended," says AznDibs, recalling his experiences as a player. "Emergent gameplay truly is amazing!"

MMC ZOMBIES PROJECT

Darkness has fallen. You and your team are holed up in a derelict shack, and you have an army of the undead on its way to claim your soul. Barricade the doors and windows, grab your best gun, and get ready to work together to survive, because it's going to be a long night!

From the "safety" of your base, you'll face waves of zombies that spawn outside and break down barricades. You'll start with a pistol, but as you play you'll earn cash to buy new guns and ammo from the chalk outlines on the walls. »»

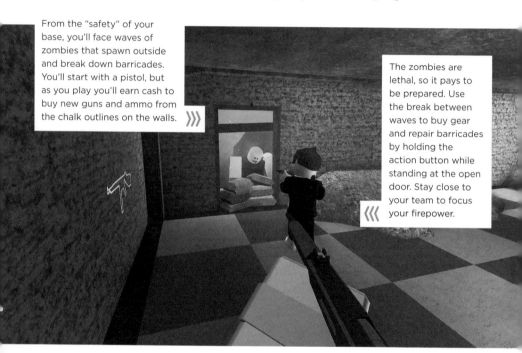

The zombies are lethal, so it pays to be prepared. Use the break between waves to buy gear and repair barricades by holding the action button while standing at the open door. Stay close to your team to focus «« your firepower.

When you reach a certain wave, a new area of the base will open up. There you'll find new weapons and gear to give you an edge against the horde, which gets bigger and «« bigger every wave.

GAME STATS

STUDIO:	Official Leek tag Fan group
SUBGENRES:	Survival, FPS, Building
VISITS:	
FAVORITED:	

QUICK TIPS

AIM TRUE
Since you have a limited magazine and reloading takes time, you need to conserve ammo if you want to survive. Aim down your gun's sights to make sure every bullet counts and increase the likelihood of deadly headshots.

MULTITASKER
You can repair your barricades while shooting, so you can keep enemies at bay while you're repairing your defenses. You can also reload and look behind you to ensure nothing creeps up on you from behind!

GETTING BETTER
If you're defeated by the zombies, you'll be incapacitated. You won't be able to move, but you can still fire your pistol to help out your team until someone revives you. Always revive teammates, but note it takes a long time.

EYE OUT
MMC Zombies Project is all about prioritizing the many threats. Find out where the horde is streaming from – possibly a broken barricade – and know where your teammates are at all times! It's dangerous to be alone.

AMBIENTOCCLUSION

Before she started making games, AmbientOcclusion didn't know so much about math, but now that she's a true programmer she recognizes its magic. Here, she explains that she enjoys Roblox because it's a place to work with others on solving hard problems that come up in development.

ON TIME
Considering it's taken a long time to add leaderboards to MMC Zombies Project, AmbientOcclusion is surprised how devoted players are to her game! "They spend a massive amount of time trying to reach high waves!" she says, explaining it can take up to three hours. "I have to say, that's a lot of dedication to a game. It shows that people are satisfied with it."

ON COMING TOGETHER
AmbientOcclusion, whose name refers to a graphics programming technique, loves the Roblox community as a place to explore computer science. "I've met wonderful people who are willing to cooperate on problems and strive for solutions," she says. "We've spent a lot of time hanging out in Script Builder games, where we show our cool creations to each other."

ON SAVING UP
"Use your knife on the first rounds," advises AmbientOcclusion. "This spares ammo for other actions, and is an effective method of attaining points in the early waves."

BLOX HUNT

Can you impersonate a waste paper bin? How about a laptop? Maybe a pumpkin? Put your skills of deception to the test in Blox Hunt, a hide-and-seek game for 10 players in which hiders disguise themselves as everyday items. Will the seekers find them before the timer counts down?

⟨⟨⟨ At the start of the game, the players are split into teams of hiders and seekers. Hiders get 30 seconds to find an object to disguise themselves as and move to an inconspicuous location.

⟨⟨⟨ If you survive a round, you'll earn tokens, which can be spent in the shop on hats, masks, and hairdos. The hiders will always be blue and the seekers always red, so you know who's who in a round.

≫ When the seekers arrive, it's time for them to find hiders by zapping suspicious objects. Seekers have to be careful, though. If they zap three non-player objects, they'll lose health.

≫ When a seeker zaps a hider, they'll jump, giving away their disguise. They can run and change into a new item, but if they're zapped too many times, they'll become a seeker too.

GAME STATS

DEVELOPER:	Aqualotl
SUBGENRES:	Humor, Simulation, Party
VISITS:	
FAVORITED:	

QUICK TIPS

KEEP STILL
Many actual objects in the game are perfectly aligned with the edges of surfaces they're on. Luckily, the game will automatically give you a few seconds after you stop moving to help you blend into your surroundings.

STUNNING SHOT
If you're discovered as a hider, the game isn't over! You also have a zap, which you can use to make a seeker fall over and give yourself a few moments to get away, but it uses a lot of your energy. Hide again as quickly as you can.

MAKE FUN
When a seeker is nearby, a button prompt will appear on the hiders' screen. Pressing the button allows them to taunt and earn bonus tokens, but it also makes a noise. If they time it wrong they might give away their disguise.

SHINY SHINY
You even have the opportunity to earn tokens in the lobby area. Use elite parkour skills to get from the spawn point to a location up a nearby wall to grab a coin worth 10 tokens. You'll need to do it before the next round starts!

AQUALOTL

A few of Aqualotl's games take inspiration from classic Roblox games, the result of 10 years of playing on Roblox. Here, he explains how he gave Blox Hunt its distinctive art style, and his trouble with focusing on a single project. Luckily, he's managed to complete a few!

ON LAUNCHING BLOX HUNT
"It was quite amazing how well Blox Hunt took off," Aqualotl reminisces. "I remember going to bed the night I released it and waking up to a game flooded with popularity. I was so excited and it inspired me to keep working on it."

ON FOCUSING
What part of development does Aqualotl struggle with? "Staying focused on one game! I have so many ideas for games that I end up abandoning one project for another." We wonder what games are gathering dust in his Studio!

ON ART STYLES
Blox Hunt's style was inspired by old BrickBattle games, which gave Aqualotl some interesting restrictions to work around. "I tried my best not to use cylinders or rotated parts," says Aqualotl "Everything was made from simple blocks."

ON FITTING IN
Here's a Blox Hunt tip from its creator: "There are some places designated to be hiding spots. Usually they are gaps in between a series of the same objects. Use these to your advantage because they help you blend in better."

RED VS BLUE VS GREEN VS YELLOW!

Four colors. Four towers. Four teams of four players. Battle high above a poisonous sea with rocket launchers, bombs, explosive crossbows, and swords. Expect explosive destruction in this modern take on an all-time classic game from the original Roblox team!

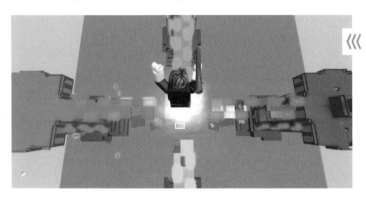

《《《 Each team of players starts on the spawn point at the back of their tower. Most of your tower can be destroyed, so don't wait to take the battle to your rivals! Eliminate them to increase the team score.

The rocket launcher takes time to reload and travels slowly, but is very destructive. The crossbow fires an explosive bolt that detonates a few moments after it hits a target. 》》

You can drop a bomb where you're standing. It's powerful; make sure you run to safety before it explodes! Use the sword for close combat, either at the middle platform or in an enemy base where you can get near opponents.

GAME STATS

DEVELOPER:	GPR3
SUBGENRES:	Fighting, PvP
VISITS:	
FAVORITED:	

QUICK TIPS

LET'S BOUNCE
In the center of the map there are two glowing jump pads and a spire. Equip your sword and leap onto a pad to launch you up in the air in order to reach the top of the spire. From here, you can jump on rivals to surprise them!

MINE SWEEPER
The crossbow can be used to lay traps for your rivals! Fire its bolts at the floor around enemies so they have no choice but to run into their explosions! It's best at medium range, because bolts drop off over super-long distances.

MISSILE COMMAND
Though they're slow, rockets are accurate and deliver splash damage, so the launcher is good for long-distance battles and destroying towers. Anticipate rivals' moves and aim at groups for maximum effect.

SET UP
Use the ladders and stairways at your base to reach the bottom of the map and jump across to reach the bottom of your rivals' towers. If you're sneaky enough, you'll be able to quietly plant bombs at their spawn point!

GPR3

GPR3 didn't expect much when he made Red vs Blue vs Green vs Yellow!, but, as he explains, that was because he wasn't making a game to attract a big audience. Sometimes you'll make a game for yourself and discover that people want the exact same things you do!

ON FINDING LESSONS
When you're learning something new, you often overlook sources of help. "I learned from scratch and it was much harder than it needed to be," he says. "There were tutorials! Eventually I found them and they helped so much!"

ON MAINTAINING MOTIVATION
What's GPR3's biggest challenge? "I'd say it's keeping a positive attitude and motivation towards your project!" Many people suffer a similar problem. "My best advice is a few hours at a time, it keeps it fresh and fun!"

ON MAKING FOR YOURSELF
Not all games come out of big ambitions. "My expectations weren't high!" GPR3 says. "I made this game because I enjoyed playing ones similar to it when I was younger and first joined Roblox. I made it to play with my friends, and to my surprise it passed 55 million visits!"

ON MAKING ROPES
GPR3's favorite plugin is Oolzedraw Toolbar: Draw/Curve Rope, which has an unusual focus. "It makes it insanely easy and quick to add realistic looking ropes, vines, and chains!"

RESURRECTION

Barricade the doors, the zombies are coming! Team up with three friends and face an onslaught of the undead. Buy new weapons, stock up on ammo, build up your defenses and collect game-changing power-ups. The zombies aren't going to stop, so it's up to you to last as long as you can!

The zombies will try to enter your base through the windows, tearing at the barriers first. If they get in, they'll come straight for you and your squad! Work together to cover every entry point!

You earn money for eliminating zombies and repairing barriers. Spend it on new weapons and ammo, and on unlocking new areas of a level.

Sometimes zombies drop power-ups. Nuke instantly eliminates all zombies, while Insta-kill gives you one-shot kills for a short period.

GAME STATS

STUDIO:	Resurrection Studios
SUBGENRES:	Survival, Horror, Building
VISITS:	
FAVORITED:	

QUICK TIPS

SIDE ARM
Don't overlook your pistol. It's not very powerful, but you'll run faster when you're holding this than with any other gun. When you're knocked down, you'll be able to fire it to cover your teammates as they revive you.

STICK IT
Conserve your ammo in the early waves by using your knifea to safely eliminate zombies who are bashing a barricaded window. You'll also be in the perfect position to collect points for repairing barricades afterwards!

LUCKY DIP
Use the Mystery Box to get a random weapon for a low price. It cuts both ways though – the weapon might be terrible, or it might be great! Just make sure you don't spend so much money you can't afford ammo.

PUNCH UP
The Pack-a-Punch machine allows you to upgrade one of your existing weapons rather than buying a new one. It costs a lot, but it'll pay for itself over time in ammo savings, and you'll be better at getting rid of zombies!

GEMINI_II

For Gemini_II, working on a team is all about communication and making sure everyone feels understood and is striving toward the same goals. Here, he explains how he ensures Resurrection's team works together well, and reveals where you can find them hidden in the game!

ON STUDIO
When you look back at all you've learned, it's easy to know how you could have made things a lot easier for yourself. "I wish I was able to go back and have a better understanding of Studio and all of its helpful features so that I could have done things more efficiently," Gemini_II says.

ON COMMUNICATION
Gemini_II's special skills are: "Communication and understanding. Having a good relationship with your fellow devs can really boost the game's drive."

ON WORKING TOGETHER
But what does a good development team look like? "It's crucial to have people who are on the same path to achieve the same goal at the best of their abilities," Gemini_II explains.

ON CAMEOS
Did you know that the Cabin map features all of Resurrection's developers on a shelf? That's not all. "The brute that spawns in is actually one of our scripters, Perhapz, and we plan on adding zombies who are all of the developers who are currently working on the game!"

ICEBREAKER!

Watch out, there's a sudden chill in the air! In Icebreaker! you'll play a series of team games in which the object is to put all your rivals on ice. Play different game modes in which you freeze foes with your breaker and keep teammates thawed to secure a toasty victory!

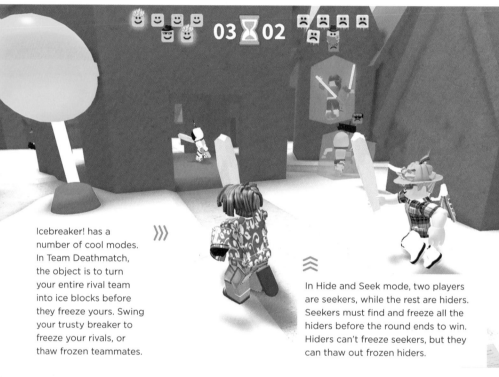

Icebreaker! has a number of cool modes. In Team Deathmatch, the object is to turn your entire rival team into ice blocks before they freeze yours. Swing your trusty breaker to freeze your rivals, or thaw frozen teammates.

In Hide and Seek mode, two players are seekers, while the rest are hiders. Seekers must find and freeze all the hiders before the round ends to win. Hiders can't freeze seekers, but they can thaw out frozen hiders.

In the Boss Battle everyone faces a giant ice-cream man who throws great balls of the sweet stuff down a hill to freeze you! Battle your way up, thawing frozen allies to reach the boss and take him down!

GAME STATS

DEVELOPER:	Cracky4
SUBGENRES:	Obby, Fighting, PvP
VISITS:	
FAVORITED:	

QUICK TIPS

ANTI-FREEZE
Frozen rivals can be used as bait for other enemies. Hide near a frozen enemy and wait for their teammates to try to unfreeze them. Hit them with your breaker before they can and you've got an even more alluring trap!

SHATTER IT
When you're first frozen, your ice block will be gray, which can't be thawed by anyone. Tap the action button to change it into your team's color, which will allow your teammates to spot and save you!

MONEY BOX
There are four crates hidden across every map. Hit them with your breaker to grab 30 coins – but make sure they don't distract you when you should be freezing foes! The other team will be looking for these loot boxes too.

COOL LOOK
Icebreaker! features many trails, emotes, breakers and faces, which can be obtained from chests bought with coins. You can also customize your in-game appearance by finding one of the full outfits hidden in the levels.

CRACKY4

Worry and doubt are a natural part of making things. Did you make the right decisions? Was it a good idea in the first place? Here, Cracky4 explains how he comes up with the concepts for his games, and how he deals with the uncertain feelings that come with making them real!

ON FINDING IDEAS
"When playing games with friends or family I'll think about why I'm enjoying myself and how I could translate those feelings into my Roblox games," Cracky4 says. "I find inspiration when doing things like outdoor activities, playing board games, and reading stories."

ON KEEPING FOCUSED
"Game development is a test of endurance as much as it is a test of creativity or innovation," says Cracky4. "Don't get sidetracked by doubt or ideas that could turn you away from your

project. When inspiration strikes, sit on the idea for a while. If after a day you're sure the idea is practical, pursue it!"

ON WORRY
It's natural to doubt a big project before you reveal it. Cracky4 felt that way about Icebreaker!. "It's easy to dwell on worst-case scenarios and write off all the hard work you've put into a game," he says. Thankfully, its release exceeded expectations. "Icebreaker! now has an incredibly loyal fan base and has outlasted many games that were released during the same period."

MURDER MYSTERY 2

Eight Innocent players. One Murderer. One Sheriff to protect them! Murder Mystery 2 is all about the thrill of survival, hunting prey, and being the hero. In each round, the Murderer is out to defeat as many defenseless Innocents as possible. Will the Sheriff come to the rescue?

A round starts off by assigning players as an Innocent, Sheriff, or Murderer. Each has a different role during the round. The more rounds you play, the greater the chance you'll be selected as the Murderer.

Innocent players simply have to survive. You'd better find a great hiding place and run when you can, because if the Murderer sees you, you have nothing to defend yourself with!

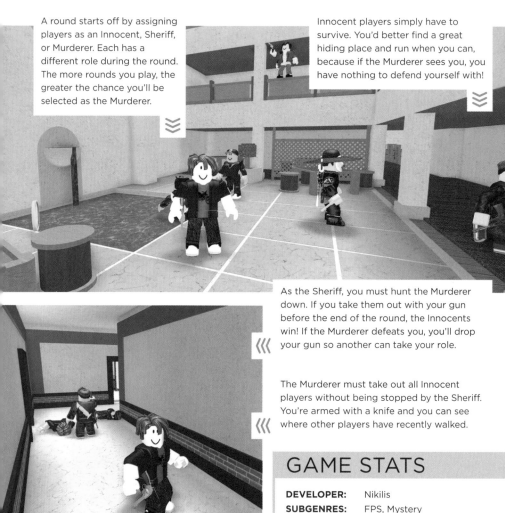

As the Sheriff, you must hunt the Murderer down. If you take them out with your gun before the end of the round, the Innocents win! If the Murderer defeats you, you'll drop your gun so another can take your role.

The Murderer must take out all Innocent players without being stopped by the Sheriff. You're armed with a knife and you can see where other players have recently walked.

GAME STATS

DEVELOPER:	Nikilis
SUBGENRES:	FPS, Mystery
VISITS:	
FAVORITED:	

QUICK TIPS

DROP SHOT
If the Sheriff is taken out, they will drop their gun and Innocent players will be able to pick it up and become the new Sheriff in town. Cunning Murderers will hover nearby, preventing it from being picked up and used against them.

PICK UP
Look out for coins. On the one hand, they will allow you to buy cosmetic effects and skins for knives, guns, and more. On the other hand, they make a loud noise, which is likely to give away your location if you're hiding.

ART OF HIDING
If you're the Sheriff or Murderer, you should aim to hide your identity from any other player and avoid becoming a target for your rival. The best way to do this is by making sure your weapon is hidden in front of other players!

PERSONAL GUARD
If you're an Innocent player, consider following the Sheriff around, because they should be able to protect you. Just make sure that the Sheriff doesn't think you're the Murderer stalking them, or else they'll attack you by mistake.

NIKILIS

When Nikilis released his first Murder Mystery game, he played it with just 10 others before going to sleep. When he woke up, he found thousands playing it! "That was a crazy experience," he says. Here, he explains how the sequel also became successful – but in unexpected ways!

ON STAYING UNDERCOVER
"Always put away your weapons right after using them to avoid getting caught," advises Nikilis. If you want to win as the Murderer you need to avoid suspicion. "Don't use them in crowded rooms," he continues. "Stealth is key."

ON UNFORESEEN CONSEQUENCES
Trading cosmetic items is massive across Roblox. As it happens, Murder Mystery 2's items have proved extra appealing. In fact, as Nikilis says, "Trading items in the game became bigger than the actual game!"

ON SECRETS
Here's something you might not have realized: every map in Murder Mystery 2 has an Easter egg. "There's a secret room in the lobby," hints Nikilis, but he'd like to keep the rest hidden. "You'll have to find them yourself!"

ON LIFE
Nikilis' fondest memories around being part of the Roblox community are all about his players. Especially, he says, "comments about how Murder Mystery 2 positively affected their lives in a big way."

ASSASSIN!

In this quickfire game of cat and cat, eight players set out to assassinate their target while avoiding being assassinated themselves. With only a knife on their side, Assassin! is all about careful planning and skillful play as each player competes to be the last hitman standing.

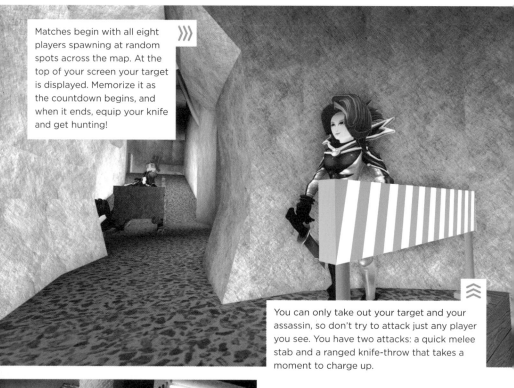

Matches begin with all eight players spawning at random spots across the map. At the top of your screen your target is displayed. Memorize it as the countdown begins, and when it ends, equip your knife and get hunting!

You can only take out your target and your assassin, so don't try to attack just any player you see. You have two attacks: a quick melee stab and a ranged knife-throw that takes a moment to charge up.

For every takedown you'll be awarded XP and tokens, which you can use to buy items like pets, effects, and knife cases that award you weapons of varying rarity. Use the crafting system to create the flashiest blades!

GAME STATS

DEVELOPER:	prisman
SUBGENRES:	Fighting, Mystery
VISITS:	
FAVORITED:	

QUICK TIPS

Your Target

PLAN OF ATTACK
Locate your first target as quickly as possible. Keep an eye on your surroundings to make sure you're not being followed, then line up your throw and eliminate your target. Do this repeatedly to be the last one standing.

STEALTHY DOES IT
An unsuspecting target is easier to take down than a nervous one, and much less dangerous! Missed knife-throws are often a dead giveaway, so try to ensure you have targets squarely in your sights.

PACIFIST
You don't need to constantly fight. Picking your battles with care means fewer takedowns, which means missing out on tokens and XP, but you might stay hidden longer and be able to win more of the matches.

SPECIAL ROUND
You'll be able to play special game types every few rounds, like Infection, where one player has 60 seconds to infect as many survivors as possible, or Free For All, which puts everyone against each other!

PRISMAN

From drawing out his ideas on paper to releasing the final game, prisman is well aware of just how many skills it takes to make a game! Here, he explains the challenge that development brings, plus some of his top tips for effective target termination.

ON SKILLS
There are many component parts to making games, from creating the art to writing code. For prisman, that's what makes them so hard to create. "If you're working solo or on a small team you'll need a wide variety of skills: coding, texturing, 3D modeling, story writing, and so on. There are more skills required to make a game than there might appear to be on first glance."

ON SUCCESS
Assassin! was one of prisman's first major projects on Roblox, but it doesn't show. "I was

very surprised with how well it was received. It took a lot of work to get the game to where it is today but it was totally worth it." Over 400 million visitors would agree!

ON GOING LOUD
Prisman was surprised to see the multitude of strategies that players adopted when they started to play Assassin!. "When I made it I thought playing cautiously would be the most effective strategy," he says. "It's a good approach, but some of the best players run all over the place and play risky!"

SILENT ASSASSIN

Somewhere out there is a ruthless assassin who's out to take down their target before escaping. Between them are 10 guards. Silent Assassin is a thrilling game in which every player has a different role and anything's possible. Will the assassin succeed? Or can the guards take them out first?

<<< A round starts by identifying the role you're playing. If you're the target, it means the assassin is after you! You're not armed, but you have your guards to protect you. Try to collect the briefcases hidden on the map for an XP and cash bonus.

<<< As a guard, it's your duty to take the assassin down with your guns before they can take out the target! If you fail, make sure you at least take the assassin down before they escape.

As the assassin, you'll be able to see the position of the target on-screen. You're only armed with a knife, but it takes just one hit to eliminate the target or any guard. Use all your guile and then escape when the deed is done!

GAME STATS

DEVELOPER:	TypicalType
SUBGENRES:	Mystery, Fighting
VISITS:	
FAVORITED:	

QUICK TIPS

ART OF HIDING
As the assassin, you can use bushes and other level features to hide in in order to get close to the target. Guards can't enter them, and they won't be able to see you either! Advance slowly to minimize your exposure to guards.

EQUIP IT
Guards have the ability to use special items. The flashlight helps you see on dark maps, while the tripwire can reveal the assassin's position when triggered – place it by a static target. The best teams have a varied item set.

SQUAD RULES
Don't forget that being a guard is a team effort. Keep a group around the target while others go out to hunt the threat down. You should be able to pinpoint the position of the assassin as guards begin to fall.

OPEN GROUND
Since the assassin can hide in bushes and around corners, you should try to keep the target in the open, so the assassin needs to break cover to attack, which should give the guards a clear shot on the sneaky assassin.

TYPICALTYPE

The distance between dreams and reality can often be wider than you hope, but as TypicalType says, there are always tools that can help narrow it. Here, he talks about how Silent Assassin wasn't as popular as he hoped, and why he'd go to space if he didn't have to follow reality.

ON PLAYERS' RESPONSE
It's always difficult to know whether the game you're making is what players are looking for, especially when you're trying to make something different. "For Silent Assassin, it has been generally well received, although the style of gameplay isn't what as many people are into as I anticipated," TypicalType says.

ON SPACE
If you could make the game of your dreams, you'd make something big, right? TypicalType thinks the same way. "I would love to make

a large-scale open-world space game, with galaxies to explore, planets you can land on and control, and space battles to take part in," he says, imagining blasting through solar systems with friends discovering new worlds.

ON TOOLS OF THE TRADE
"One of the most useful tools for Roblox development is the ability to use plugins," says TypicalType, referring to the packages of code available in the Roblox plugin library. "They add functionality to Studio and make it easier to create games the way you envision them."

BED WARS 2

Are you ready to defend your island from all challengers? Are you prepared to take the fight to them? In Bed Wars 2 you defend your spawn point from your rivals while trying to take theirs out! Collect resources, buy powerful gear, build your defenses and battle your way to victory!

<<< Your island features your team's shop, iron and gold resource nodes, a chest, and a spawn point. Nearby, you'll see other islands, where you'll find valuable resources. Buy blocks from the shop and build a bridge to reach and claim them.

≫ The shop sells building blocks, armor, and weapons for fighting, tools to break blocks, and upgrades. These items cost gold, iron, diamonds, and emeralds, which generate at different node points.

≫ Your spawn point is your most important location – you won't be able to respawn after it's been destroyed, and you'll lose the game. Your objective is to eliminate all rival teams by destroying their spawn points and defeating them!

GAME STATS

DEVELOPER:	jandel
SUBGENRES:	Fighting, Exploration, Tycoon
VISITS:	
FAVORITED:	

QUICK TIPS

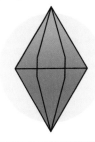

ATTACK A BLOCK
Encase your spawn point in blocks to help protect it from attackers. They'll only be able to break through if they come equipped with pickaxes first, giving you more time to return to your base to stop them!

GREEN FOR GO
Emeralds are the most valuable resource in the game, and they give you access to dynamite and other powerful items. Be ready to fight, though, because every other team will be trying to get their hands on them!

SAVE IT
Avoid defeat at all costs! You'll lose any equipment you had and your rival will be able to grab resources you were carrying. You can use the chest at your base to store resources and keep them safe in case you die.

FLASHBACK
Once you have acquired some diamonds, make sure you buy a teleorb. This wonderful device lets you teleport back to your spawn point, away from danger or to instantly defend an enemy attack!

JANDEL

The original Bed Wars was jandel's first-ever project. After having fun playing Natural Disaster Survival with some friends, he decided to investigate what it would be like to make a game on Roblox, and he ended up making Bed Wars. Here, he explains how it changed his life!

ON ASKING QUESTIONS
Jandel wasn't afraid to ask for help when he began exploring Roblox. "I connected with every developer I could and asked them questions relating to game design, marketing, and the Roblox platform."

ON JUMPING IN
After learning about making games with Roblox, he decided to try it. "I decided to dedicate two weeks to scripting Bed Wars, and two weeks later I uploaded the project as Bed Wars Beta." A week later, it was on the front page of Roblox.

ON CHANGING LIVES
Bed Wars' success was a big surprise. "It was completely wild. I severely underestimated how much Roblox would impact my life. Bed Wars has changed my life immensely. I was able to travel to San Francisco and meet everyone at Roblox and pursue my passion for game design."

ON SAVING UP
Here's jandel's tip for pro Bed Wars play: "The biggest tip I have is to build bridges to emeralds right at the beginning of the game so you can buy the team upgrades!"

THE MAD MURDERER 2

Look out, there's a killer on the loose! This game of hunter and hunted pitches a single Murderer and their knife against 13 innocent players and one Sheriff. Or perhaps you'll play one of the super-fun alternative modes. No matter which you choose, you'll need skill and cunning to win!

In The Mad Murderer 2, the Sheriff is the only player with a gun. It's up to them to find and defeat the Murderer! If the Murderer defeats the Sheriff, they'll drop their gun so another innocent player can become Sheriff.

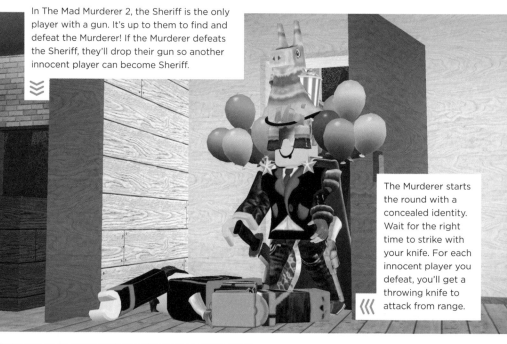

The Murderer starts the round with a concealed identity. Wait for the right time to strike with your knife. For each innocent player you defeat, you'll get a throwing knife to attack from range.

Tile Smasher is a fun mode in which you must throw knives at the tiles beneath your rivals' feet, sending them falling to their doom! Be the last one standing to win. In Free for All, everyone's out to defeat each other.

GAME STATS

STUDIO:	MAD STUDIO
SUBGENRES:	Fighting, Mystery
VISITS:	
FAVORITED:	

QUICK TIPS

IN THE WALLS

The Murderer can destroy certain objects and access areas of the map that other players can't, such as vents. Use them to navigate the levels in secret before jumping out to take your many victims by surprise!

GATHER QUEST

Each of the maps is scattered with special purple orbs that you can obtain. If you collect enough, you'll have the chance to collect a special cosmetics chest, which can contain rare weapon skins for knives and guns.

GUN CAMP

The Sheriff's gun drops when they're defeated. It'll remain in its dropped position for a short period before it respawns elsewhere. Innocent players can make a dash for the dropped weapon, but it could be dangerous to try...

SINGLE OUT

It can be difficult for innocent players to know which player is the Murderer if they aren't openly attacking any Innocents. Keep an eye out for players who seem to be following you, and look to see if they're holding a knife.

LOLERIS

Every challenge loleris has faced has given him something valuable to learn from, but he takes the most inspiration from immersing himself in other people's creations, whether books, cartoons, movies, or games. Here, he explains how that's what makes his games special.

ON WHAT SETS HIM APART

He doesn't believe he has special skills that elevate him above other devs. "I'm fairly certain most of us write more or less the same code," he says. "What really sets us all apart is how we perceive the perfect game concept and what experiences we want to share with the players."

ON ALWAYS LEARNING

In making The Mad Murderer 2, loleris felt he was lacking in some development skills and wanted to improve, because even with six years of experience, he knew he had lots more to learn. "I was impressed by how I managed to use new technologies. With new knowledge I feel prepared to take on ideas I had to turn down a few years back!"

ON GOOD EASTER EGGS

"We like to add secrets openly, in hard-to-find places, such as hidden in concealed shortcuts or subtle ledges that let you access new areas," loleris says. One is a window in the Office map that can only be broken by the Murderer. "Only the most agile players will figure out a way to get into that room!"

BLOODFEST

If you're in the mood to face a cavalcade of the undead, BLOODFEST is just the thing! Pick a class and team up with your friends to take them out! Then buy better weapons so you can face the next wave. Can you survive all 10 waves of the undead and face down the end boss?

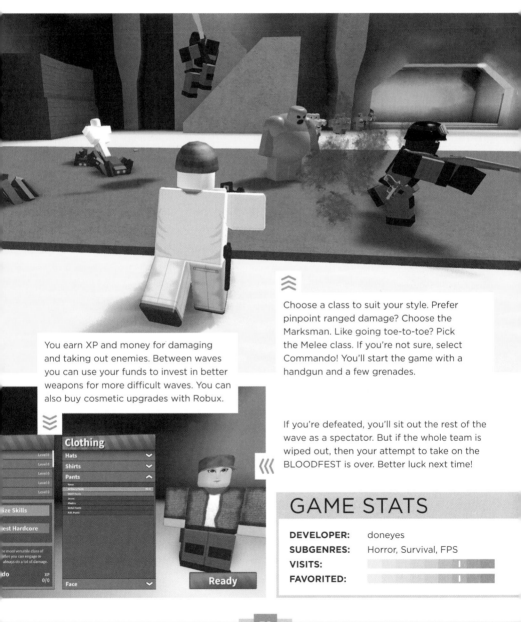

Choose a class to suit your style. Prefer pinpoint ranged damage? Choose the Marksman. Like going toe-to-toe? Pick the Melee class. If you're not sure, select Commando! You'll start the game with a handgun and a few grenades.

You earn XP and money for damaging and taking out enemies. Between waves you can use your funds to invest in better weapons for more difficult waves. You can also buy cosmetic upgrades with Robux.

If you're defeated, you'll sit out the rest of the wave as a spectator. But if the whole team is wiped out, then your attempt to take on the BLOODFEST is over. Better luck next time!

GAME STATS

DEVELOPER:	doneyes
SUBGENRES:	Horror, Survival, FPS
VISITS:	
FAVORITED:	

QUICK TIPS

FIRST AID
Don't forget you have the ability to heal yourself. There's a short cooldown period before you can use it again, so keep an eye on your health and your surroundings and always try to refill it when it's sitting below halfway.

TAP OUT
Most enemies have a weak point – usually, but not always, the head. The rocket launcher enemies, for instance, have a fuel tank on their backs which explode when you hit it! Aim for the weak point to deal extra damage!

OPEN SEASON
The maps are dense with interconnected corridors, so you'll often find enemies approaching from many directions. Try to avoid open areas as these are particularly dangerous – enemies can easily surround you.

CLASS WAR
As you progress, you can buy weapons for each class, so you're not tied to your starting weapon or class. Look at your team and see what they're missing – if there's no Melee specialist, consider buying a fire axe, for example.

DONEYES

BLOODFEST's success has been life-changing for doneyes, since it's led to three internships at Roblox and moving to California! Here, he talks about why he loves Roblox, how he struggled to keep his projects small enough to make, and how he learned to better control their size.

ON GETTING INTO ROBLOX
Doneyes first fell in love with Roblox because of the way everything was physically simulated. "It created these unique sandbox experiences."

ON MORE WITH LESS
Remembering when he started to make games, doneyes wishes he'd learned sooner to keep his ambitions smaller. "I think a lot of us want to make these huge immersive experiences, but you have to learn how to do more with less," he says. "Even now I find that my quick three-month projects end up taking three times longer."

ON ROBLOX'S COMMUNITY
"My favorite part about the Roblox community is how accepting people are of new games," says doneyes. "There's no other platform where you can release a game with next to no advertising and have it accumulate literally millions of plays."

ON MANAGING GAME SCOPE
"Don't get caught up on the small details," advises doneyes. "Make the core game loop playable first and then start fleshing it out. It's easy to lose track of the big picture when you're too focused on the details."

SPEED RUN 4

Don't you find sometimes that you just have the need for speed? When you get that feeling, Speed Run 4 is just what you require: a game all about racing your friends across a series of maps of giant platforms and instant-death falls. It's time to leave them all in your dust!

))) Make your way to the starting line. As soon as you cross it, you'll get a burst of speed. It's time to get running! You'll see every other player in the map also racing with you. Can you keep up?

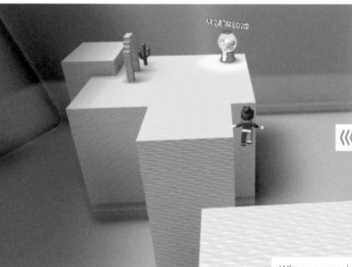

Follow the course, jumping to new platforms. If you fall off you'll need to restart! You'll get an extra long jump at the end of a ramp, helping you get farther. Watch out when you can't see ahead, you))) might jump into the void!

When you reach the end you'll be able to collect a star and be awarded with gems. Go through the arch to progress to the next))) course – it's time to do it all over again!

GAME STATS

DEVELOPER:	Vurse
SUBGENRES:	Racing, Obby
VISITS:	
FAVORITED:	

QUICK TIPS

FLY AWAY
The key to getting across complex platforms is air control! No matter what speed you're flying through the air, you can stop or turn immediately, giving you the chance to pull out of a bad jump or nail a landing.

PRESS START
As soon you enter the next course, you can push forward to start running again. It'll keep your pace up, and help you stay ahead of friends! Your total time is tracked in the top-right corner, so you can compare your progress.

CHANGE TRACK
Stars unlock alternative play modes and are activated from the lobby. Zombie Mode places zombies in the courses as additional hazards, and equips you with a gun to shoot them as you run! It's tricky to master!

SPACE RACE
Check out different dimensions in Speed Run 4! These collections of courses have different visual themes, but you need codes to unlock them in the menu. Here's one from the developer himself: "moon."

VURSE

Vurse knows Speed Run 4 is a simple game, but he was confident it'd be a success because its speedy challenge was just what players were after. Here, he talks about what it took to make a game that's so focused, and about the place where his love for Roblox started!

ON WORKING WITH TEAMS
Good leadership skills are vital when you're making games, as Vurse has found. "My secret weapon in game development is the ability to negotiate and sway other developers to work alongside me in collaborative projects. Since everyone has expertise in certain fields, bringing the right people together to create a good game is important."

ON FOLLOWING YOUR NOSE
Vurse finds it best to think broadly when creating games, and to not get bogged down by the little things. "Roblox projects come together best when you follow gut instincts and refrain from drawing out meticulous details into project-halting escapades," he says.

ON FAVORITE MEMORIES
When he looks back at his best times on Roblox, Vurse remembers the original Welcome to ROBLOX Building game. "I was building tall towers and private rooms that only friends could visit, and launching myself from the tower to secret hidden Builderman spots on the map where he would say secret messages."

SHARKBITE

Face the terror of the deep blue sea in this game of sailor versus shark! 14 players navigate the ocean in boats while one other plays as the shark, patrolling the depths and waiting for a chance to snap them up. The survivors have guns. The shark has teeth. Which will rule the waves?

))) The survivors get a minute at the start of the match to get their guns ready and sail their boats into position. Their task is to either avoid the shark for the entire round, or to work together to take it out first. Neither option is easy.

))) The shark is huge, fast, and lethal. It only needs to crash into a boat to smash it, and any player who gets between its teeth is a goner! The shark player can see blue trails coming from boats and red trails from survivors in the water.

Stranded mode puts every player on a single raft, giving the shark a juicy target. But being close together combines the survivors' firepower! Chest Chase mode spawns a chest in the ocean for a brave player to dive in and collect.

GAME STATS

STUDIO:	Abracadabra_Studio
SUBGENRES:	Fighting, Exploration, Monster
VISITS:	
FAVORITED:	

QUICK TIPS

SPEEDBOAT
Boats can just about stay ahead of the shark when going at full speed, but you'll need to know where it is to stay away from danger. Listen for the shark's music, watch for the pulse that shows its position, and zoom your view out.

SURFACE TENSION
The shark is most effective when it's taking survivors by surprise, so stay in deep water, locate a target, and use the boost to rapidly surface before the survivors are able to spot you and run away. Dive again right afterwards.

LARGE TARGET
The Double Shark mode is extra fun, pitting two sharks against survivors. But shark players must remember that they share a health bar between them. Twice the sharks means survivors have a bigger total target to shoot at.

LOOK OUT
If the shark treated you to an early, watery grave and you're awaiting the next round, get up to the top of the lighthouse for a grandstand view of the watery carnage! It's just as fun even when you're at a distance.

OPPLO

While opplo was able to make games on his own, he knew that working with other developers would mean more productivity and better releases. That's why he got together with Simoon68 and formed Abracadabra_Studio.

ON MAKING MISTAKES
Don't worry about errors, opplo advises. "It's important for beginners to know making mistakes is normal. Even to this day I spend weeks on small issues that are hard to fix!"

ON COOPERATION
"It was surprising to see players working to save others from the shark," opplo reveals. "I saw a whole group of players on one boat fighting the shark and it inspired us to create the Stranded mode where everyone is stuck on a single raft fighting to win the round together!"

ON BUOYS
"Keep an eye out for four buoys on the surface of the water," says opplo, as they can detect the shark! "If you're a survivor you'll be safest near a buoy, if you're a shark you can destroy buoys so players don't know where you are!"

ON DREAM GAMES
He would love to make a game of physics contraptions. "Where you build vehicles and spaceships with friends while exploring, completing puzzles and competing for prizes. Oh, and pets too, that's always important!"

THE REALLY EASY OBBY!

Some obbys are very hard, but this colorful obstacle course is great for gathering your friends together and embarking on a race to the top. Every new challenge is different and takes you higher and higher. Jump, run, climb, and solve puzzles. Just don't look down!

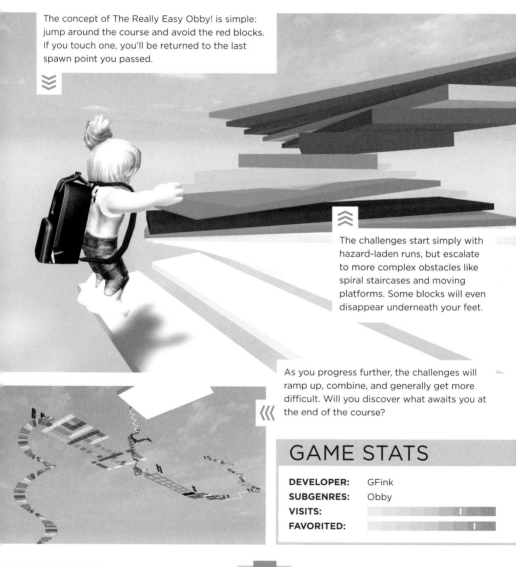

The concept of The Really Easy Obby! is simple: jump around the course and avoid the red blocks. If you touch one, you'll be returned to the last spawn point you passed.

The challenges start simply with hazard-laden runs, but escalate to more complex obstacles like spiral staircases and moving platforms. Some blocks will even disappear underneath your feet.

As you progress further, the challenges will ramp up, combine, and generally get more difficult. Will you discover what awaits you at the end of the course?

GAME STATS

DEVELOPER:	GFink
SUBGENRES:	Obby
VISITS:	
FAVORITED:	

QUICK TIPS

SPEED RUN
Can you beat The Really Easy Obby! in under six minutes? To do so, you'll need to avoid almost all time-consuming errors, but it's possible! If you succeed in your efforts, you'll be rewarded with a rare game badge.

PANORAMA
A wide view can really help with some of the obstacles. You can change the FOV setting while playing, which zooms the viewpoint in and out so you can see more of the obstacle that is coming next.

GOOD OLD DAYS
Without wanting to spoil the surprises the end of the course, let's just say that one attraction is like a museum of Robloxian history, incorporating structures from some of the classic Roblox games.

LOST TIME
Once you get a little way through the stages, don't forget to look back at where you came from! You may see players struggling to beat what you've just been through, and you may even be able to navigate back to help them!

GFINK

GFink has learned a huge amount since he started making The Really Easy Obby! all the way back in 2011. Here, he shares some of the wisdom he's learned, and why his games have to be good enough for him to play before he's ready to promote them to the rest of the Roblox community.

ON CODING
When GFink was first making The Really Easy Obby! he didn't know Lua. "I didn't code any of the tools in the game," he says. "The last obstacle was to get a parachute and glide down to the winner's area. When the game became popular, I was flooded with messages about how to beat this last obstacle. Because I didn't know how to script at all, I just replaced it entirely!"

ON REPLYING
GFink loves to reply to messages people send him. "I think it's great to be able to talk to anyone and everyone regardless of what they have to say, encouraging or critical."

ON ADVERTISING
"Showing people your game doesn't work by itself," says GFink, who bought lots of advertising to promote The Really Easy Obby! in its early days. They didn't work in bringing in lots of players though. "My game wasn't any good then. What I didn't realize is that if I genuinely enjoy playing the game, there's a good chance everyone else will too. The game being advertised needs to be enjoyable too."

THE FLOOR IS LAVA

In The Floor is LAVA, you'll find yourself with your friends in a small map that's about to be flooded with hot, flowing, molten rock! Look for the high ground, climb up as far as you can, and try to survive the flood for 30 seconds. Then start the fun all over again in the next round!

⟨⟨⟨ Each round has a few seconds before the lava arrives. Look around for the highest point and run for it. You should make it off the ground before your feet get hot!

⟨⟨⟨ For every win you'll be awarded 10 points. You spend them in the lobby on cosmetic items that you can take into the game, such as an edible burger, a spray can to paint decals on walls, and a hoverboard.

In the Lava Escape levels, the lava will keep getting higher and higher, and you'll need to find the ladders to get to the next level. Climb and run – don't stop until you reach the top. ⟩⟩⟩

The lava will steadily rise as the timer ticks down. Buildings and objects in contact with it will turn black and burn away. Will they last long enough so you'll survive the round? ⟨⟨⟨

GAME STATS

DEVELOPER:	TheLegendOfPyro
SUBGENRES:	Obby, Survival
VISITS:	
FAVORITED:	

QUICK TIPS

HEAD START
It won't make you many friends, but don't worry about using other players to get away from the lava! Use the opportunity to jump on their heads to reach the highest spots! Selfishly think of them as stepping stones to success.

HOT FEET
When objects like walls and floors burn, they'll break apart and may end up floating in the lava. If you're pretty skillful, you'll be able to jump from object to object and may be able to find a way back to higher ground.

QUEUE JUMP
When everyone rushes for the same ladder, you might find yourself falling off or having to wait your turn. You don't have to follow the crowd – there's usually more than one way to higher ground, so take a look around!

STUDY PERIOD
There are lots of different levels to play in The Floor is LAVA, but try to memorize the best places to run in each map. The more you play a map, the better you'll know it and the higher your chances of survival the next time round.

THELEGENDOFPYRO

For TheLegendOfPyro, making things isn't the challenge, it's making creative things. As he says, "Anyone can cook, but it depends what you cook. That makes all the difference!" Here, he explains why he was surprised his game became so popular, and why he loves Roblox.

ON FIRST SUCCESS
TheLegendOfPyro's expectations for The Floor is LAVA were low. "It was my first attempt at a round-based game and I wasn't experienced," he says. But its innovative dynamic lava proved to be popular! "I had no idea it was going to be this big of a success and did not expect it to be played by people all around the world."

ON PLUGINS
There are lots of tools out there that can help you make games, but TheLegendofPyro wasn't aware of them when he got started. "I wish I

knew about plugins," he says. "For anyone out there trying to be a developer, plugins will help tremendously, and will let you do things you can't do as easily with regular Studio."

ON MAKING FRIENDS
"My fondest memory of playing Roblox games is probably just chilling and hanging out with people," says TheLegendOfPyro. "It's one of the things that's so unique to Roblox. In fact, I've actually met one of my good Roblox friends in real life, so it goes to show the kind of connections this awesome platform can create."

TOWER BATTLES

You might know tower defense games, but have you ever played a multiplayer one? In Tower Battles, you'll place towers along a lane of marauding zombies to stop them from reaching the end, saving money to send zombies over to your rival before they do the same to you!

Play Tower Battles alone, in cooperation with friends, or against others in versus matches. In each, your aim is to survive as long as you can. The loser is the first team to let through enough zombies to destroy their health bar!

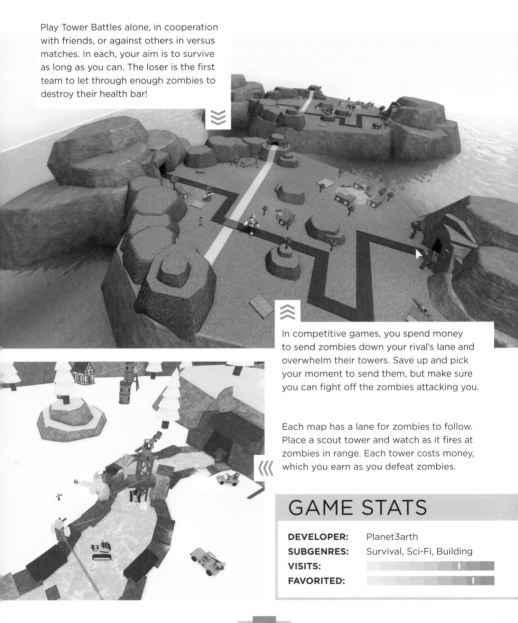

In competitive games, you spend money to send zombies down your rival's lane and overwhelm their towers. Save up and pick your moment to send them, but make sure you can fight off the zombies attacking you.

Each map has a lane for zombies to follow. Place a scout tower and watch as it fires at zombies in range. Each tower costs money, which you earn as you defeat zombies.

GAME STATS

DEVELOPER:	Planet3arth
SUBGENRES:	Survival, Sci-Fi, Building
VISITS:	
FAVORITED:	

QUICK TIPS

  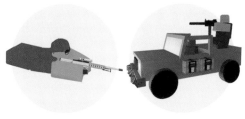

ARMY UPKEEP
Make sure you spend your credits between games to purchase and equip new towers. Each offers brand-new strategies for you to explore, but you can only take four different tower types into each battle, so you're slightly limited.

CROWD CONTROL
Tower placement can be trial and error to get the best results. Place a cryo-gunner, which slows zombies and makes them bunch up, next to a fragger, which delivers splash damage that hits all zombies in a large radius at once.

I SEE YOU
Hidden zombies can only be attacked by maxed-out scout towers, or snipers that have the radio upgrade purchased. Snipers can only be placed on the tops of buildings, but they can have extraordinary map-wide range!

ACT FAST
If it looks like the zombies are about to break through your defenses, use a patrol – an SUV that drives up the lane and crashes into any zombies until its health runs out! It's expensive but might save the day on a tricky level.

PLANET3ARTH

Ideas are easy, right? They just pop into your head, and then you make them! But when it comes to making games, ideas are not quite so simple. Here, Planet3arth explains how sorting the good ideas from the bad can be one of the most challenging parts of being a Roblox developer.

ON GOOD IDEAS
Not all successful developers think they're special. "I pursued a good idea when it came to me," says Planet3arth. "If there's a grounded thought process behind an innovative idea, all it takes is time and effort to make it real."

ON SCRAPPING BAD IDEAS
Knowing if an idea is good is the hard part! "I rushed into making part of an idea before I had the whole vision of the game," Planet3arth says. "I'd get three weeks into building and realize, 'What the heck am I doing?! This is a bad idea!'

Knowing when to scrap a bad idea and when to pursue a good one is a difficult skill to master."

ON WINNING
Here's his top strategy tip: "It's important to know how to sabotage your opponent by taking advantage of flaws in their defenses."

ON THE LAST WAVE
"A hidden wave of enemies can come after you beat the game," says Planet3arth. "It reveals a bit of Tower Battles lore by revealing who patient zero was, and what they turned into."

SUMMONER TYCOON

In Summoner Tycoon, you're no wizened old wizard, you're a mighty summoner, commander of an army of heroes who will go to battle for you! Build your laboratory to make them stronger, and summon ever more formidable warriors to do your bidding. Can you collect them all?

Earn crystals to summon heroes. At first you can only summon from the first tier; at level 10 you can summon from the second, increasing the chance of getting rare, legendary, or even exotic heroes! Equip up to three from your inventory.

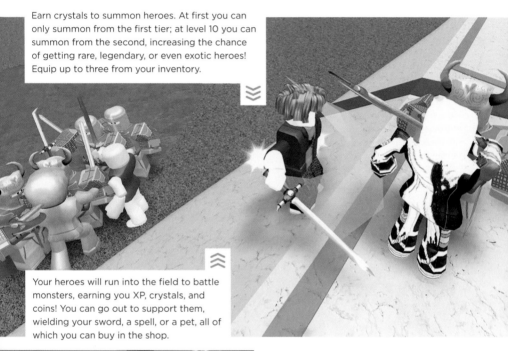

Your heroes will run into the field to battle monsters, earning you XP, crystals, and coins! You can go out to support them, wielding your sword, a spell, or a pet, all of which you can buy in the shop.

Spend coins on your laboratory, buying equipment that will increase your heroes' stats. Summon more heroes, equip the best ones, and sell duplicates to afford more and more expensive components.

GAME STATS

STUDIO:	Albatross Studio
SUBGENRES:	Tycoon, Fighting, Building
VISITS:	
FAVORITED:	

QUICK TIPS

ORDER UP
Use commands to control your heroes. They may be powerful, but they're not very clever and can forget who they should be attacking. If you want support on the battlefield, use Defend to keep them around you while fighting.

TOP DROP
When everyone in the map has slain a few hundred monsters, a super strong boss monster appears. Beware! It can smite you easily, but if you can kill it, it may drop unique heroes and items to power up your existing roster!

VITAL STATISTICS
Each hero has different characteristics. Don't just focus on attack: health ensures they stay out in the field for longer, and speed means they'll find a new target quickly and be able to attack them faster.

AROUND AGAIN
After level 30 you can rebirth, which means starting all over again at level one. You keep heroes and equipment and get a Rebirth Soul which buys super-powerful heroes, spells, and weapons, increasing your starting power.

COOLBULLS

Before he started making Summoner Tycoon, coolbulls looked at other games on mobile and Roblox that had similar mechanics to the super-popular Clone Tycoon 2. Here, he explains why research is so important to his process and how other games inspired him!

ON PLAYING OTHER GAMES
Looking at what players like is a great way to get ideas. "I spend a lot of time playing and thinking about what I will be making next," says coolbulls. "Whenever a new game hits the front page I try it out, watch YouTube videos, and also read the comments so that I can understand the game from not only my own perspective, but also from the players' perspective."

ON OTHER PLAYERS
When coolbulls thinks about what game to make, he imagines his players and what they're after, rather than what he wants to play. "If I want to make a popular game, I have to consider what other people want in it, rather than just thinking about what I want to see. Creating something popular requires a user-first mindset."

ON RETENTION
Once you have a game that players are interested in playing, the next challenge is keeping them engaged. "To me it's the most challenging aspect," says coolbulls. "It requires countless hours of thinking about the design, marketing, and any upcoming updates."

OPERATION SCORPION

Two teams of operatives go up against each other in this exacting game of teamwork and skill. Get in, plant the bomb and defend it, or play the opposite side, taking out the other team before they can carry out their mission. This is precise, tactical Roblox action at its finest!

Invade is the main game mode. Teams take turns to carry and plant a bomb at a point on the map. One player carries the bomb, and once planted, the team must defend it until the countdown finishes.

You'll level up and earn credits as you play; visit the Customization menu to buy weapons and fit attachments to improve what you have. Consider how they affect your playstyle.

The opposing team must stop the bomb by defusing it or wiping out the bomb team once the countdown starts. Which objective they choose will influence how you defend it.

GAME STATS

STUDIO:	MAXIMILLIAN
SUBGENRES:	FPS, Mystery
VISITS:	
FAVORITED:	

QUICK TIPS

ART OF NOISE
With a lot of ground to cover on every map to get to objectives, sprinting is important, but you make a lot of noise and alert your rivals to your presence. Use the crouch to move quietly when close to an objective.

SET DOWN
When planting the bomb, you'll need to hold your position for a few seconds, unable to use your weapon. Only start when you know the area is clear of enemies, or if you have a squad covering your back as you plant it.

PRO-OPERATIVE
Avoid presenting your rivals with a big target to shoot at by leaning around corners, and get into the habit of hovering over the aim button as you move so you can shoot quickly. The quicker you are, the better your chances.

LINE DANCE
When you win a match, don't forget to show off and gloat in the post-match winner line-up! Use your lean, turn, and other movement controls to pose your military men and show the enemies exactly who defeated them!

CBMAXIMILLIAN

Lots of the biggest Roblox games are built on teamwork. Here, cbmaximillian explains how he manages the team behind Operation Scorpion, and how sometimes aiming for perfection can cause a complex project like this to go astray. But talent can always pull it back together again.

ON SPECIALIZATION
For cbmaximillian, Operation Scorpion's quality is down to one thing: "Every member of the MAXIMILLIAN team is assigned to their specified talent," he says. "By using this technique we're able to create a spectacular product that is a combination of many people's mastery."

ON RECRUITING
To collect such a talented team, cbmaximillian looks for how people react to the game. "The ones whose eyes shine when they see the prototype, the ones who get things done and

offer what could be better, and the ones who try beyond what's expected. Recruiting great people saved a lot of management headache."

ON RECEPTION
"I thought I was putting out a game that was unlike anything on the platform," says cbmaximillian. "I expected players to be blown away. I was right to an extent." The team struggled to meet the style and technical level they aimed for, missed updates, and the game stagnated. But after going back to the drawing board, the game found its feet with new content!

BRICKBATTLE SHOWDOWN

Be a demolitions expert in Brickbattle Showdown, the game which puts you into frantic battles with your friends while the world around you falls apart! Fight with bombs, a rocket launcher, a slingshot, dodgeball, and more, in this explosive entry into Roblox's classic brickbattle genre.

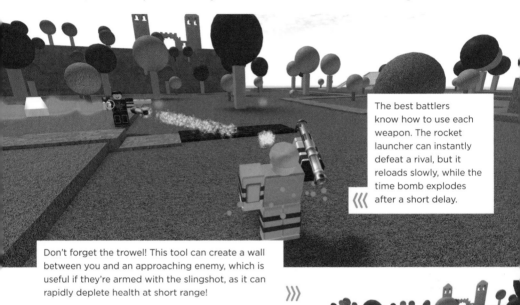

The best battlers know how to use each weapon. The rocket launcher can instantly defeat a rival, but it reloads slowly, while the time bomb explodes after a short delay.

Don't forget the trowel! This tool can create a wall between you and an approaching enemy, which is useful if they're armed with the slingshot, as it can rapidly deplete health at short range!

The dodgeball is a bouncy orb of devastation. It travels at immense speeds and can deplete half its targets' health! Try to keep at a distance. If you're in a close combat situation, use a sword.

GAME STATS

STUDIO:	Silver Fin Studios
SUBGENRES:	Fighting, Exploration
VISITS:	
FAVORITED:	

QUICK TIPS

DODGE THIS
Time bombs seem underwhelming at first. But not if you throw a deadly dodgeball at them! The bomb will bounce away at speed and explode, taking targets by surprise! You'll have to get good at switching weapons.

AIM HIGH
The trowel's walls aren't only good for defending against attacks. You can also use them to reach areas that you can't jump to! Place the blocks to use them as a step to reach high spots or to give yourself a vantage point.

SWITCH IT
Everyone's favorite weapon is the rocket, but don't insist on sticking with it after firing. It takes a while to reload, so switch to another weapon in the meantime and then back to the rocket launcher when it has ammo.

BRING IT DOWN
If your rivals have holed themselves up at the top of a tower, why not bring them down to your level? Plant a few time bombs around each floor and watch the building collapse underneath them, allowing you to pounce!

AQUALOTL

What should a game look like? How should it feel? What do you want your audience to think about when they play? These are questions that Aqualotl thought about a lot as he made Brickbattle Showdown. Here, he explains the little visual details he put into it that make it special.

ON FINDING A STYLE
It can be tough to find a visual style that makes sense for your game. But Aqualotl found an ideal look for Brickbattle Showdown. "It's designed to look like you're in a simulation," he says. "The lobby is the real world and in-game is fake! That is why everything flickers like a hologram and your player shatters upon death."

ON LITTLE DETAILS
Aqualotl added an extra layer to its simulation style that was inspired by the early days of Roblox. "UI elements for Brickbattle Showdown

when in game are designed to look very similar to early Roblox UI," he says.

ON PLEASANT SURPRISES
"Brickbattle Showdown turned out much better than we thought," says Aqualotl. "The game was very polished and gave me the nostalgic feel of playing old brickbattle games I wanted."

ON PRIDE
The game didn't have the instant success he was hoping for, but success isn't everything. "We're still very proud of the progress it has made."

HOSTILE SKIES

Ah, those magnificent Robloxians in their flying machines! In this WWII flight simulator you'll take to the skies as either the Allies or Axis in a series of historically accurate and realistically simulated planes. Dogfight your way to victory, sending all challengers crashing!

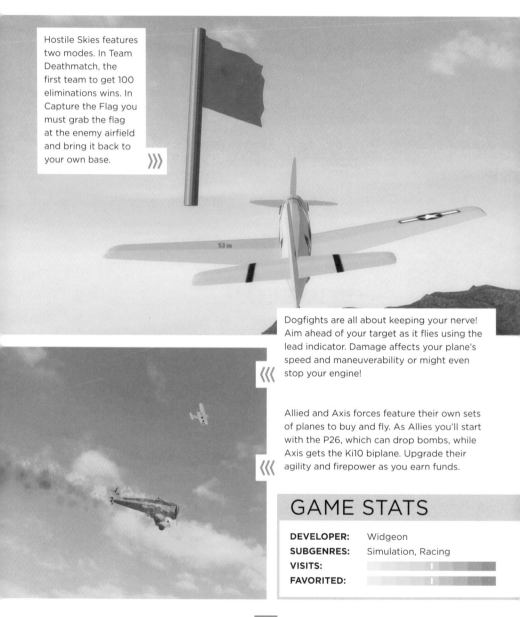

Hostile Skies features two modes. In Team Deathmatch, the first team to get 100 eliminations wins. In Capture the Flag you must grab the flag at the enemy airfield and bring it back to your own base.

Dogfights are all about keeping your nerve! Aim ahead of your target as it flies using the lead indicator. Damage affects your plane's speed and maneuverability or might even stop your engine!

Allied and Axis forces feature their own sets of planes to buy and fly. As Allies you'll start with the P26, which can drop bombs, while Axis gets the Ki10 biplane. Upgrade their agility and firepower as you earn funds.

GAME STATS

DEVELOPER:	Widgeon
SUBGENRES:	Simulation, Racing
VISITS:	
FAVORITED:	

QUICK TIPS

MAX OUT
Going as fast as possible in a plane isn't always the best idea. They have a tendency to fall to pieces! Watch for overspeed warnings, and reduce your airspeed by turning down your throttle, climbing to a higher elevation, or turning.

WATCH YOUR SIX
Got a bogey on your tail? Use all your maneuverability to move your plane around and make yourself a hard target. A teammate may swoop in and take out your pursuer! Good teams always look out for each other.

HAPPY LANDING
If your plane has taken damage, you can make repairs by landing at your faction's airfield. If your plane has landing gear, make sure it's lowered before you land, and use the brake to stop, or you could do more damage!

FLYING ACE
Rack up at least three eliminations without being defeated to earn a streak. Streaks are the key to earning the big bucks, which you'll need to buy better planes and advanced upgrades – longer streaks mean more money.

WIDGEON

Widgeon's first-ever Roblox game, way back in 2010, was all about planes. "It was some form of airport game where you flew planes from one island to another," he says. So Hostile Skies is in some ways a return to where he got started! Here, he explains how he made it.

ON MODULES
It can be rewarding to create tech for a specific game, but it's a better idea to make it work for lots of different games, according to Widgeon. "For example, I created a projectile module for my game Aegis and modified it to work with Hostile Skies."

ON SIMULATION
Hostile Skies uses real aerodynamic data to simulate its planes. "Every plane is simulated as realistically as possible using wind tunnel data from a real NACA 0018 airfoil."

ON FLYING ACES
Widgeon put some features into the maps to test pilots. "There are tunnels you can fly through," he says. "Completing the tunnel without crashing is quite the feat." But he can't understand one thing: "New players don't try to avoid crashes in head-on situations!"

ON FANTASY
But Widgeon made changes to reality to make Hostile Skies more fun. "It's scaled down to 1/4, meaning your character is only 1.25 studs tall, and the P26's wingspan is only six studs wide."

ROBLOX BATTLE (2018 EDITION)

Let's sink into a warm bath of Roblox nostalgia! Roblox Battle was released by the Roblox team back in 2012, where its destructible levels took the platform by storm. Now you can dive back into the action with this updated version, which still features the classic retro look and timeless explosive fun!

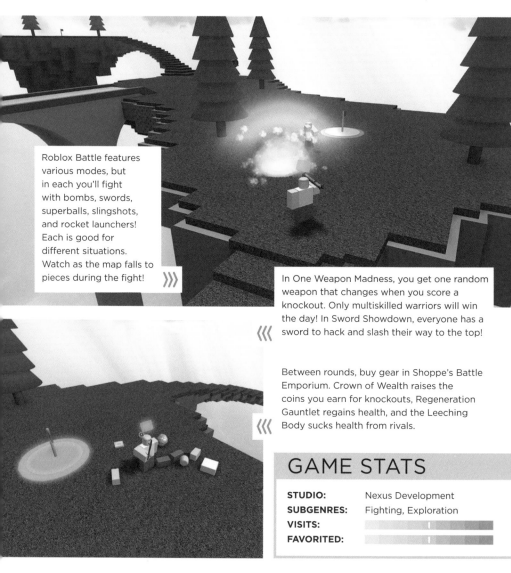

Roblox Battle features various modes, but in each you'll fight with bombs, swords, superballs, slingshots, and rocket launchers! Each is good for different situations. Watch as the map falls to pieces during the fight!

In One Weapon Madness, you get one random weapon that changes when you score a knockout. Only multiskilled warriors will win the day! In Sword Showdown, everyone has a sword to hack and slash their way to the top!

Between rounds, buy gear in Shoppe's Battle Emporium. Crown of Wealth raises the coins you earn for knockouts, Regeneration Gauntlet regains health, and the Leeching Body sucks health from rivals.

GAME STATS

STUDIO:	Nexus Development
SUBGENRES:	Fighting, Exploration
VISITS:	
FAVORITED:	

QUICK TIPS

KING OF THE HILL
Head for the high ground for a distinct advantage over your lowly foes! Your weapons have increased range when you're aiming downhill. Bombs are especially effective when rolled down the slope towards your rivals!

FLIGHT PATH
Take note of the trajectory the slingshot and superball take through the air as you fire them. They don't fly straight like most bullets. Learn how to aim and they can be the most formidable weapons in the game.

FLOOR IT
Try to aim the rocket launcher at the ground near your rival's feet so they're hit by its splash damage. If you aim directly at them and miss, the rocket will fly straight past them and you won't do any damage.

TIRED OUT
Don't bunny hop your way around the maps, as you'll get exhausted after a few jumps. It could spell your doom if you need to leap up a step to get away from enemies! Reserve your jumps for these emergencies.

THENEXUSAVENGER

Roblox Battle is free for anyone to copy and use as a template for their own games, because TheNexusAvenger thought other developers would find it useful as a showcase of good Roblox tech! Here, he explains some of the other challenges he faces in making games.

ON DIVERSITY
TheNexusAvenger's favorite thing about Roblox is its scale. "I have met young kids, fellow college students, and a few developers over 50 who play and develop," he says. "People of different backgrounds, cultures, and languages."

ON LANGUAGE
Roblox is international, so translations help everyone enjoy it. But as TheNexusAvenger says, "Translations aren't easy, since some words are region-specific. There wasn't a direct Spanish translation for 'Dodgeball,' for example…"

ON TESTING
TheNexusAvenger is proud that this was his first game to not have any major bugs on launch! "That's because several QA tests helped break major components of the game," he explains, meaning fixes were made before release.

ON PUSHING
"Flinging people over the edge is a way to get knockouts," says TheNexusAvenger, though you won't earn coins! "The sword is probably the best weapon for this, and also provides a speed boost while walking."

FISTICUFFS

You, sir! Yes, you! Let us put our fists up and indulge in some light Fisticuffs for our entertainment! Punch your way to the top of the leaderboard in a team battle game that's all about punching your rivals so hard they fly out of the level. It's a knockout!

⟨⟨⟨ To win, you need to get KOs, which you earn by delivering a mighty punch that launches rivals out of the level! But you can only perform that punch once you've softened them up by knocking their health down.

If you've been punched enough to lose your health, you're in danger of being KO'd! But if a rival hits you again, you might be lucky enough to have your flight broken by a wall, which will keep you in the level, ready to ⟨⟨⟨ punch again.

Power-ups appear during a round – punch them to activate. Green heals you, yellow gives your next punch extra power, dark blue blocks the next hit you receive, red allows you to briefly move faster, and light blue will temporarily slow your target.

GAME STATS

DEVELOPER:	Ozzypig
SUBGENRES:	Fighting, Humor
VISITS:	
FAVORITED:	

QUICK TIPS

GLOVES OFF

Earn Mustaches for KOs and wins, and use them to buy new punch types. There are lots to choose from, including Critical Punches, Double Punches, and Lifesteal. Try to create the best combo of punches.

ON GUARD

The block move is useful to avoid being hit and taking damage, but successful blocks will also stun your attacker, leaving them unable to move or attack. Take advantage and land as many punches as you can.

LINE UP

If you see a red disc floating in the level, it's your chance to do some ranged damage. You can punch the disc towards your rivals. If it hits them, it'll deliver a lot of damage! But beware as they can do the same to you!

BREATHING SPACE

Feeling battered and bruised? Head to the Time Out area for a breather. You can't be harmed here, but you won't heal either. Take a moment to rest your fingers and assess the battle before jumping back into the fray!

OZZYPIG

Ozzypig isn't afraid to cut a good idea out of a game if it's not working. But instead of throwing it in the trash, he stores it away for future games. Here, he explains why, what kind of VR game he'd love to make, and the secret to being a successful Roblox developer!

ON CUTTING

"You'll never be able to put all your ideas into a project, so cut, cut, cut!" says Ozzypig. "Your best ideas are refined through playtesting and debugging. If a feature isn't up to snuff, don't be afraid to shelve it for another day."

ON MAGIC HANDS

If Ozzypig could make any game, it'd be in VR. "Where you can cast spells with your hands. Perhaps you're fighting off hordes of monsters, or going head-to-head with another spellcaster. Like fencing, except fantastic and magical."

ON LEARNING

What's Ozzypig's secret? "If I told you, then it wouldn't be a secret anymore!" he jokes. "It's a solid education. Take time to sit down and really get to know the software and the coding language you're using and nothing will be impossible."

ON BAITING

Ozzypig recommends being sneaky. "The cooldown for blocking punches is long, so bait your opponent's block to leave them vulnerable, and then you can get risk-free hits on them."

FRAY

This hardcore PvP first-person shooter is the real deal. Equip perks to tip the balance in your favor, or unleash killstreak abilities that call in stealth bombers to drop explosives over the map. Fast, smooth, and responsive, Fray is the ideal place to prove your battle skills!

Team Deathmatch is the classic mode, a balanced game of teamwork and skill. You'll earn killstreaks for eliminating rivals without being taken out; get three and you can send up a UAV drone to reveal enemy locations.

In Domination you'll capture zones, which add points to your team's total. Stand in the circle to make it yours, then defend it from the enemy or move on to capture the next while they scramble to keep up!

As you defeat your rivals, you'll earn points that help your team claim victory and gain you ranks that unlock new perks, killstreaks, weapons, and skins.

Zombies mode is a full-on zombie defense game in which you must survive waves of undead walkers. Barricade windows, open up new areas of your base, and buy powerful weapons that'll see you through the night.

GAME STATS

STUDIO:	Bad Skeleton
SUBGENRES:	FPS, Simulation
VISITS:	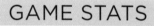
FAVORITED:	

QUICK TIPS

CHART MAP

Learn the maps thoroughly. This will help you memorize routes to each objective, choke points where you can lie in wait for your rivals, and convenient overhangs that are perfect for turning into a sniper's nest.

GUN SHOW

Set up your best weapons with attachments. You can change the type of sight that you aim through and adjust their stability, range, and other attributes. You can also swap paint jobs with skins you've unlocked by playing the game.

FRAG OUT

It's easy to forget your grenades when you're in the middle of a gunfight. However, they're useful for throwing around corners when you're pinned down to create an opportunity to run, and they can thin out a crowd easily.

ADDED BONUS

Equip one of the many perks to support your unique playstyle. If you like running and gunning, Focused lets you reload while sprinting. Nickleback gives you five extra points for every elimination and hit.

JANDEL

Fray is a very focused game, because it's about one thing: fast FPS action. But jandel started out having trouble keeping his games focused. Here, he explains how he learned to stay on track, what his intentions were for Fray, and what surprised him most about how people play it.

ON STAYING ON COURSE

When he was starting out, jandel often lost sight of his original ideas. "They quite often diverged a lot," he says. "It's important to plan out a theme fully and only diverge a little, otherwise you end up re-scripting your systems to accommodate new ideas that don't work with your plan."

ON AUDIENCES

Jandel had a specific intention when he set out to make Fray. "We wanted to create an FPS game targeted at an older audience," he says. Fray has gone down well, but jandel's especially pleased with one aspect. "We had expectations that the community would take our Rthro model well and it's great to see that everyone did!"

ON COMPETITION

It's often hard to know how your game will be played by your audience. Jandel was most surprised by how competitive Fray's players are. "We recently started supporting all the different leagues people created for the game," he says. "It's amazing seeing people create their own communities within our game and watching them compete!"

ISLAND ROYALE

What better way to start a game than to jump out of a floating bus with 99 other players? Island Royale challenges you to be the sole survivor. Scavenge weapons and equipment from buildings around the land, build a base to defend, and take on all challengers to be the victor!

⟨⟨⟨ Up to 100 players will be competing to be the winner in each game, and you all start in the bus flying across the island. Jump out when you're ready, and freefall down towards an area that looks safe.

You'll find weapons, ammo, and other items scattered around or in chests. Pick them up but note you can only carry six items at a time. Make sure you're carrying a good range of gear! ⟩⟩⟩

Every piece of scenery, from trees to walls, is destructible! Smash your way to a rival who's holed themselves up, or collect wood, brick, and metal, which ⟨⟨⟨ you can use to build a base.

A damaging perimeter draws in as the round continues! Over the course of the match, the safe area gets smaller and smaller; step ⟨⟨⟨ outside it and you'll begin to lose health.

GAME STATS

DEVELOPER:	LordJurrd
SUBGENRES:	Fighting, Exploration, Survival
VISITS:	
FAVORITED:	

QUICK TIPS

TEAM CHAT
You can team up with your friends in a squad of four, or pair up with one other buddy, helping you keep track of where you are. Make sure you communicate to form plans and work together to be the last team standing.

QUALITY MATTERS
The rarity of a weapon affects the damage output, so always swap your gun for a Rare, Epic, Legendary, or Mythic variant if you're lucky enough to find one! Rarer weapons might have other increased stats too.

SECURE MEASURE
You can construct walls inside a building for extra protection against invading rivals. Go upstairs and block the stairway. Don't let your guard down as they will be able to break through eventually, but you'll hear them coming.

CURE ALL
Don't neglect your shield! Drink Mini Potions to take your shield up to 50% and the Shield Potion to top it up to 100%! If your shields are full, make sure you have some health items like bandages to heal you too.

LORDJURRD

Big ideas take a lot of work to complete, and knowing exactly what you can achieve can often be difficult. That's something LordJurrd used to struggle with, as he explains here, along with how he managed to build a big following for Island Royale before it was even released!

ON MARKETING
Making your game is one thing. You also have to let people know about it! "Before Island Royale was released and once it reached a state I was comfortable with, I teased it to build up a following," says LordJurrd. "It blew up! I began posting weekly teasers and new things."

ON GETTING EARLY FEEDBACK
Hype built fast before the game was released. "Players got excited, sending me ideas and feedback," says LordJurrd. "In the end, the game turned out better than I had imagined."

ON BEING REALISTIC
It can be difficult to know what's realistic on big projects. "When I first started developing games I would set unreasonable goals," says LordJurrd. "My games were far too big for the knowledge and skill I had, and I had to learn how to work on ideas that I could manage."

ON BEING AMBITIOUS
But while being realistic is important, LordJurrd notes you have to aim high to improve yourself. "You won't ever get better at things unless you push yourself a little!"

POLYGUNS

Lock and load your own way in this super-fast, sci-fi shooter. Run swiftly through a set of detailed maps, aim true, and earn yourself a K/D ratio to be proud of. Then cash in your winnings on weapons and armor that support your playstyle, from speedy shotgunning to sneaky sniping.

When you first play Polyguns, you'll start off with a standard set of armor and weapons. Don't worry! You're still lethal. Your Hornet-ASC assault rifle is easy to handle, while your Raptor-ASC is accurate.

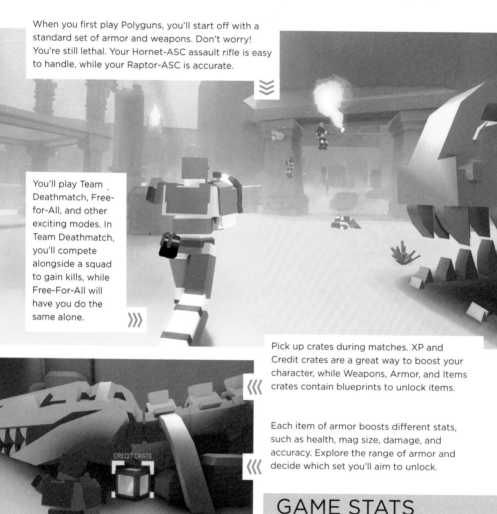

You'll play Team Deathmatch, Free-for-All, and other exciting modes. In Team Deathmatch, you'll compete alongside a squad to gain kills, while Free-For-All will have you do the same alone.

Pick up crates during matches. XP and Credit crates are a great way to boost your character, while Weapons, Armor, and Items crates contain blueprints to unlock items.

Each item of armor boosts different stats, such as health, mag size, damage, and accuracy. Explore the range of armor and decide which set you'll aim to unlock.

CREDIT CRATE

GAME STATS

STUDIO:	Mailbox Games
SUBGENRES:	FPS, Sci-Fi, Survival
VISITS:	
FAVORITED:	

QUICK TIPS

RECOVERY
Your shield will recharge very quickly, so you can escape with a very low shield and be back into the fray within a few seconds. Be sure to chase your rivals so that they don't have time to let their shields recover.

OVERWATCH
Equip the Turret item and place them around the zone in choke points or elevated locations to create a safe area around your spawn points! Turrets have a medium range, so they're weak against snipers shooting from a distance.

COME AGAIN
Stay away from enemy spawn points! Players respawn invincible for a few moments and can fire their weapons, so enemies will be able to get an easy elimination if you camp around their spawn area.

HIGH JUMP
If you prefer to play as a sniper-type, use the Jet Boots or Jetpack to reach an elevated position to snipe from and avoid close-range attacks. The best rifle is the Rail Overlord, which can KO opponents in a single shot.

ENDORSEDMODEL

You wouldn't know it, but EndorsedModel says all his projects are the result of lots of failures and mistakes. But that's how he learned to make better games! Here, he explains why understanding game design is so important to creating fun mechanics that stand the test of time.

ON DESIGN
EndorsedModel's understanding of good game design is one of his most important skills. "It's not enough to look at what other people have done and clone it," he says. "You need to understand both why decisions about mechanics and map design were made, and how they impact gameplay and the game loop. Once you understand, it's easier to apply those concepts to your own game in a meaningful way."

ON LOOPS
Even though he understands game design,

making fun games is still his biggest challenge! "Coming up with an engaging loop that attracts new players, while retaining long-term players, takes time and experimentation," he says.

ON DEDICATION
The way so many Polyguns players have stuck with the game has surprised EndorsedModel. "The support, excitement, and dedication of some of our players surpassed our expectations!" he says. "Some of them even started to make their own unofficial leagues and groups based around the game."

ZOMBIE HUNTER

The zombies are coming, and it's time to team up with a platoon of fellow hunters to take them on. Zombie Hunter will throw increasingly intense waves of the shambling walkers at you. It'll take teamwork and all the bullets you can spare to survive to the bitter end!

The first wave of zombies will feature standard green walkers. They're just enough for your starting weapon, a simple pistol, to handle. As you progress, you'll face more and more types, from flaming fire to tank zombies.

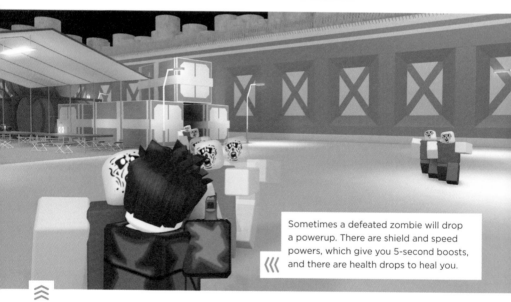

Sometimes a defeated zombie will drop a powerup. There are shield and speed powers, which give you 5-second boosts, and there are health drops to heal you.

Your health recharges between waves and, if you are taken out, you'll be respawned at the start of the next wave. If the whole team is eliminated in a wave, the game is over and you'll be sent to the lobby. Who got the highest score?

GAME STATS

STUDIO: Explosive Entertainment Studio
SUBGENRES: Fighting, Survival
VISITS:
FAVORITED:

QUICK TIPS

UP CLOSE

The knife is a powerful weapon, but it puts you in danger as you have to get close to zombies to land a hit. Only use it as a last-ditch defense when you're surrounded by dozens of the undead walkers!

TURN COAT

If you're in the lobby while a game's in progress, you can press a red biohazard symbol to play against your team as a zombie! You can't do damage but it's fun to experience the game from the other side.

CHARITY CASE

Don't always grab powerups for yourself. Sometimes it's better that a teammate gets to use them, especially if they're low on health. Or maybe if they'll be more useful later in the round, you could leave them entirely.

BIGGER GUN

Make sure you keep buying new guns and gear. The starting weapons don't deal enough damage to cope with the strength and numbers of zombies you'll face in the later waves, so you'll definitely need an upgrade!

EXPLOD_E

Roblox is a social gaming platform, where people come together from all over the world to play and make games. That's exactly what's made it so fun for Explod_e to make Zombie Hunter, from watching how it's played to taking on the community's feedback and ideas.

ON MOVEMENT

Explod_e is very proud of Zombie Hunter's animation. "Unlike most round-based shooting games on Roblox, we decided to take a different route from the minimalist animation style," he says. "We wanted to create a fun and somewhat realistic experience for our players."

ON FEEDBACK

Explod_e has found talking to players makes development better! "As I got more and more involved with Zombie Hunter's community and their ideas, my motivation improved drastically."

ON SELFLESSNESS

Explod_e was surprised to see players socializing in Zombie Hunter. "When I thought about the type of players who would play, I concluded they'd be selfish in ensuring they survived rounds. However, players were more considerate and involved in ensuring all players were able to survive."

ON GLOBAL SCALE

"The idea that I am able to communicate and collaborate with developers and like minds from all over the world is astonishing to me!"

ACHIEVEMENT CHECKLIST

You've bested all opponents in arenas of combat, but have you truly mastered the art of combat? To set yourself above the competition once and for all, see how many of these exclusive achievements you can earn with your fighting prowess. Can you complete them all?

REACH LEVEL 100
MURDER MYSTERY 2

Become a master of the blade by reaching the maximum level of 100. You'll need to dispatch legions of competitors to reach this lofty standing, but as long as you aim true and stay hidden, this should be a breeze.

MEET THE DEV
FLEE THE FACILITY

Nothing will impress your fellow Robloxians more than being the savior of a superstar Roblox dev. To achieve this badge, you'll need to meet MrWindy in-game and ensure that you can escort him from the facility safely!

COMPETITIVE TOP 10
ASSASSIN!

Form is temporary, class is permanent, or so the saying goes. Prove your exquisite form at least by occupying one of the top 10 leaderboard spots in Assassin! when a season ends.

10 ELEMENTS UNLOCKED
ELEMENTAL BATTLEGROUNDS

Become one with the elements and master 10 different varieties in Elemental Battlegrounds. Not only will you earn an awesome badge, you'll strike fear into any mage that dares oppose you.

NO GOING BACK
NOTORIETY

Take the initial steps to becoming a feared criminal by completing your first heist in Notoriety. Money, power, and infamy await you on the other side. Just make sure you don't make too many enemies.

DEFEAT BOSS
FIELD OF BATTLE

The bigger they are, the harder they fall. Meditate on this mantra when you come up against a gigantic boss enemy in Field of Battle. Team up with your friends to defeat one and you'll be rewarded with this badge.

PARTY WOOT WOOT
PARKOUR TAG!

This badge doesn't exactly demonstrate your hardened battle abilities, but it is all kinds of fun. Start dancing with a bunch of players until a dancefloor appears to unlock this achievement.

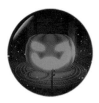

SEEKER VICTORY!
BLOX HUNT

Being a combat master is not just about hitting the hardest, it's about spotting every danger. Get your hands on this badge by finding all hidden players and winning the round as a seeker.

THE FALL OF JACK
RESURRECTION

You'll cleave through dozens of reanimated monstrosities in Resurrection, but nothing will be able to prepare you for the abomination that is Jack. Destroy him to unlock this super rare badge – less than 1 in 1000 players have it!

EARTHBOUND
DODGEBALL!

Add an extra level of difficulty to a round of Dodgeball! by constraining yourself to ground level. If you can win a match without jumping once, you'll be awarded this unusual achievement.

HARDCORE
SUPER BOMB SURVIVAL

Simply surviving shouldn't be satisfactory for a combatant of your caliber. Head to the Super Bomb Survival options screen and turn on hardcore mode, then make it to the end of a round to earn even greater renown.

CLOSE CALL
SILENT ASSASSIN

Not everything will go your way in battle, but the most important thing is to survive. While playing as the assassin, eliminate your target and escape the map with less than 10% of your health remaining.

KILL ALL SPAWNS!
BED WARS 2

Work together with your team to take out every spawn point for the opposing enemy teams, ensuring that no one will be seeking you out for revenge. That'll hand you an easy win and a shiny new badge.

THE ULTIMATE GUN
THE MAD MURDERER 2

This ultra-rare achievement requires dedication and persistence. First you'll need to obtain all 10 numbered guns, then craft them into an extremely rare unobtainium-tier gun. It's the ultimate weapon!

UNTOUCHABLE
EPIC MINIGAMES

Consistency is key to unlocking this achievement. You'll need to win 10 minigames in a row, which will depend on your skill and a little bit of luck to get some favorable games in your run.

BEAT MIRROR MODE
SPEED RUN 4

You'll be a pro at the frustratingly hard Speed Run 4 once you've beaten all 30 levels, but do you know the courses so well that you can do them backwards? Give it a go and beat them all in Mirror Mode to get this badge.

THE LAST SHOT
SHARKBITE

One could simply survive a round of Sharkbite by not being eaten, but the best warriors take the fight to the shark. Work with your fellow stranded survivors to kill the shark, and land the last blow to see it off.

BLOXXER
BRICKBATTLE SHOWDOWN
Awarded only to the finest brickbattlers around, this badge is reserved for those competitors who have been able to eliminate over 250 enemies, and have won more games than they've lost.

MVP
HOSTILE SKIES
Being the best means being better than everyone else, including your teammates. To attain this badge, you'll need to end a round with a higher score than the rest of your team – it doesn't matter whether you win or lose.

SAVED BY THE BALL
ROBLOX BATTLE (2018 EDITION)
This badge requires exquisite timing, nerves of steel, and a bouncy superball. You'll need to time a throw of the superball at exactly the right moment in order to detonate a rocket in mid-flight. Explosive!

HEADSHOT!
FRAY
Master the art of ranged combat to have a chance of obtaining this achievement. Execute a single headshot with any gun to unlock it, but don't rest until you've wiped out the remainder of the enemy team!

SOLO VICTORY!
ISLAND ROYALE
Sure, you can win a match of Island Royale in pairs, trios, or squads, but you have to share the plaudits if you do that. Getting a solo win on the other hand, means the hard-fought victory was yours alone!

LOSER MVP
DODGEBALL!
No matter how good you are, you can't win them all, especially with teammates to drag you down. Learn how to be honorable in defeat by collecting this badge for being the best player on the losing team.